This book belongs to

EXCITING CROCHET

EXCITING CROCHET

A Course in Broomstick and Tunisian Crochet

Muriel Kent

A David & Charles Craft Book

Line illustrations by Lyn Blake of Line Design
Photography by Tony Griffiths, Photography 2000

British Library Cataloguing in Publication Data

Kent, Muriel
   Exciting crochet: a course in broomstick
   and Tunisian crochet.
   1. Crocheting
   I. Title
   746.43′4   TT820

   ISBN 0-7153-8922-X

Phototypeset by Typesetters (Birmingham) Ltd,
Smethwick, West Midlands
and printed in Great Britain
by Butler & Tanner Limited, Frome
for David & Charles Publishers plc
Brunel House   Newton Abbot   Devon

Distributed in the United States by
Sterling Publishing Co. Inc,
2 Park Avenue, New York, NY 10016

CONTENTS

LIST OF COLOUR PHOTOGRAPHS

INTRODUCTION

Tunisian and Broomstick Crochet have been grouped together in this book for various reasons. Many people who have been crocheting for years have never heard of these variations, both of which place the loops on to a needle or hook and then the loops are cast off so that two rows, 'there and back', are necessary to complete the stitch row. In *A Complete Crochet Course* I introduced both Tunisian and Broomstick Crochet with a lesson on each and a few patterns. This book is the result of the interest which that created and the demand by readers for more ideas and patterns.

At one time when teaching classes I always insisted that students learning Tunisian and Broomstick Crochet must learn the traditional crochet first, but after taking several mixed ability classes I found that beginners could start by learning Tunisian and Broomstick and the basic crochet stitches could be picked up as required. Basic crochet stitches are explained in Appendix 1, but if you find them difficult the edgings can always be knitted.

A Complete Crochet Course was written for complete beginners to follow through and teach themselves and this book is written in the same way. If you have never crocheted before it does not matter – start at the beginning and providing you follow the instructions you cannot go wrong.

For the projects in this book I have used unusual wools, not found in every wool shop, from small producers such as the Black Sheep Shop at Aylsham in Norfolk, the hand-dyed wool from Gloria Watson in Dorset, hand-spun wool from Ray Napier of Neal Street, London WC2 and Creativity of New Oxford Street, London W1. There are many craftspeople all over the world producing exciting hand-spun yarns. Experiment and, provided you prepare tension (gauge) squares as described on page 49 to ensure a good fit, you can use a wide variety of yarns.

I have included one stitch which looks like Tunisian but it can only be worked 'in the round' and has been used to create a pair of gloves (see design 6). A Berber woman in Marakesh taught me this stitch and I would like to take the opportunity of recording it.

Terms for American readers are given in brackets and do not apply to English crochet.

Left-handed Crocheters

I find that people who are left-handed can often manage without reversing the instructions. The Tunisian hook is held in the right hand and the yarn is placed round the hook by moving the left hand. Handicapped people with a certain immobility of the right hand can support the hook in the lap and let the left hand do the work.

Muriel Kent
Chichester
1987

ABBREVIATIONS & TERMS

UK		USA	
ch	chain		
sl st	slip stitch		
dc	double crochet	sc	single crochet
tr	treble crochet	dc	double crochet
htr	half treble	hdc	half double crochet
dtr	double treble	tr	treble
tr tr	triple treble	dtr	double treble
quad tr	quad treble	tr tr	triple treble
TR tr F	Tunisian raised treble front		
TR tr B	Tunisian raised treble back		
st	stitch		
tch	turning chain		
lp	loop		
inc	increase		
dec	decrease		
tog	together		
patt	pattern		
sp	space		
RtrF	raised treble front	RdcF	raised double crochet forward
RtrB	raised treble back	RdcB	raised double crochet backward
gr	group		
cl	cluster		
Ts	Tunisian simple		Afghan st
Tht	Tunisian half treble		
Ttr	Tunisian treble		
Td	Tunisian stitch double		
Tdtr	Tunisian double treble		
Ttr tr	Tunisian triple treble		
Tp	Tunisian purl		
Tdp tr	Tunisian dropped treble		
Tss	Tunisian stocking stitch		
Tb	Tunisian bobble		
	Cast off		Bind off
	Catch down		Tack down
	Tension		Gauge
	Yarn round hook		Yarn over
	Slip		Skip
	4 ply		Sport
	Double Knitting		Knitting Worstead
	Aran		Fisherman
	Chunky		Bulky

TUNISIAN CROCHET

TUNISIAN CROCHET

Tunisian Crochet is worked with a long hook which resembles a knitting needle with a hook at one end. The method of working is rather like a combination of knitting and crochet, retaining the last loop of the crochet stitch on the needle and then working a return row to cast off (bind off). This makes a firm thick fabric which has a double knitting quality, so it is useful for jackets and blankets.

It is a very old craft, probably practised before knitting and weaving. It has been called Russian Work, German Work and Afghan Stitch and there is evidence that it has even been practised in Peru. The Victoria and Albert Museum in London have a sample given by Kay Shuttleworth which she bought from a harem in the Middle East. The Berber shepherds are supposed to have practised it, but on holiday recently I saw many Berber shepherds and not one of them was doing Tunisian Crochet! In the Middle Ages when knitting was a Guild Craft and practised by the men at the end of an apprenticeship, the apprentice boys had to complete a selection of garments in thirteen weeks and one of these was a blanket in Tunisian Knitting. Could this perhaps have been what we now call Tunisian Crochet?

In Victorian times all kinds of needlecrafts were an accepted way for a refined gentlewoman to earn a living. Queen Victoria promoted lace crafts, employing a Franco Irish lady called Mademoiselle Reigo de la Branchardière to teach all her daughters and grand-daughters, and a photograph of Queen Victoria shows her holding a Tunisian hook and a piece of crochet. The Victorians made rugs and blankets on very long hooks which were made in four parts and screwed together. It

must have been very hard, tiring work especially when the project was nearly completed and became very heavy. They called the stitch they used idiot stitch because it is so easy and repetitive, but the stitches explained in this book are far more interesting! These long hooks were also made in plastic in the forties and fifties and one lady I met in a Women's Institute Group said that during the Second World War she had made sixteen blankets in Tunisian stitch. Quite a feat!

In America Tunisian Crochet is called Afghan Work, and the basic stitch Afghan stitch. It is extremely popular for knee rugs and now all knee rugs are called 'Afghans' whatever the stitch used or however they are made. The basic stitch is worked in a neutral colour and wide panels are embroidered with cross stitch and crocheted together. There seems to be no stitch variation at all.

I hope this book will introduce Tunisian Crochet to a much wider audience and perhaps start a revival of interest in it. It is very relaxing to do and it is possible to obtain many exciting textures and patterns in a very simple way. In half an hour a beginner can learn to make a coloured fabric which resembles weaving.

Stitches and designs are also given for a double-ended hook. The hooks originate from France (see list of suppliers in Appendix 4) but when travelling in France I have been unable to get any information on how they use them. The stitches and garments are entirely my own ideas, I hope you like them and perhaps will design some of your own. I would be very interested to hear from any readers who have seen patterns for double-ended hooks.

TUNISIAN BASIC TECHNIQUES

Beginners should read the book with yarn and hook in hand and progress slowly following the instructions. You will be pleasantly surprised to find how easy it is and how quickly you learn. Experienced crocheters can skip the instructions they are familiar with.

Yarn

It is much simpler to learn with a thick yarn such as Aran (fisherman) or chunky (bulky) in a plain bright colour. When the stitches have been mastered in a thick yarn it is then possible to try a variety of types and thicknesses of yarn and every one will give an entirely different effect.

Choosing a Hook

Hooks are available in sizes from 2.50mm to 7.00mm in England and from F to K in America. Sizes up to 10.00mm (15 wood) may still be available in shops with old stock. The larger sizes are very good for chunky (bulky) yarns. As a guide, hook sizes for Tunisian Crochet should be about two sizes larger than for ordinary crochet. A hook which is too fine will give a

hard stiff fabric. Double-ended hooks are available in sizes up to 7.00mm (K).

Working Method

Every stitch is made of two rows. The stitch pattern is crocheted from right to left and the second row is a cast off (bind off) or return row from left to right and is the same for nearly every stitch. When using textured or mohair yarns the texture or fluffiness tends to come out on the wrong side, so sometimes the wrong side is more attractive than the right side. If this is so make the garment up inside out!

Begin by Tying a Slip Knot

All crochet stitches begin with a slip knot on the hook.
1 Hold yarn in the right hand with the end hanging down.
2 Grasp end of yarn with the left hand and with the right hand wind it once round the first two fingers of the left hand.
3 Insert hook into circle of yarn and pull loop through circle and onto the hook.
4 Pull long end of yarn to tighten loop on hook.

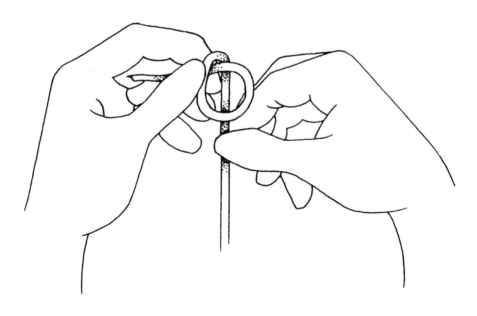

Fig 1

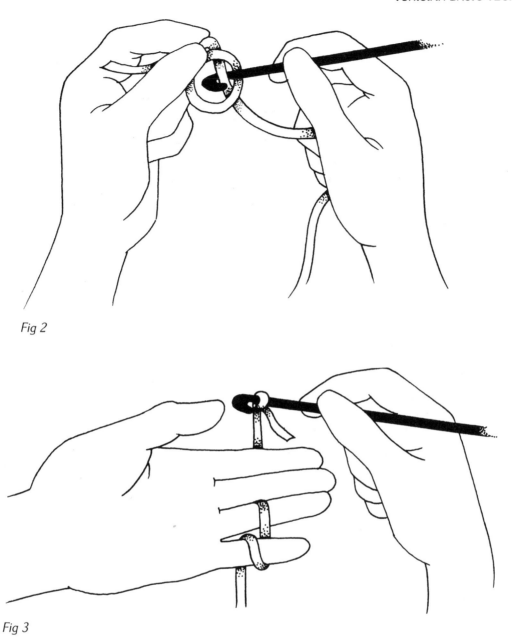

Fig 2

Fig 3

Holding the Yarn

Knitters who usually hold the yarn with their right hand find it difficult to change and hold it in the left for crochet but it is necessary for the left hand to control the yarn, thus allowing the latter to flow easily and smoothly from hand to hook giving speed and an even tension. With a little practice it becomes automatic, however difficult it may seem at first.

1 Hold the left hand with fingers extended and palm uppermost.

2 Hold hook and slip knot in the right hand.
3 Bring yarn between the third and fourth fingers of the left hand, over and behind the fourth finger.
4 Continue over the third finger, passing to the back between the third and second finger.
5 Relax hand, turn over and the yarn will fall over the first and second fingers.
6 Grasp the slip knot with the first finger and the thumb.

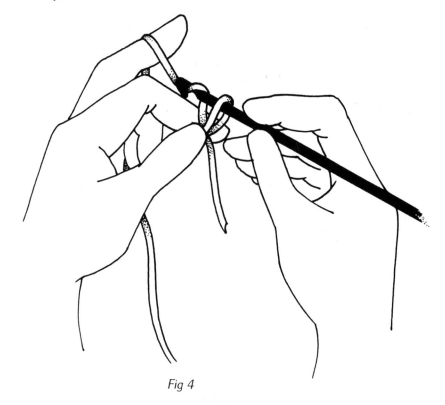

Fig 4

Making a Chain (ch)

1   Hold hook in the first finger and thumb of the right hand, supporting the hook underneath with the third finger.
2   Hold the slip knot with the first finger and thumb of the left hand. The second finger is raised to hold the yarn in position for working from the hook.
3   Move hook under the yarn and pull a loop through, yarn round hook (yarn over).

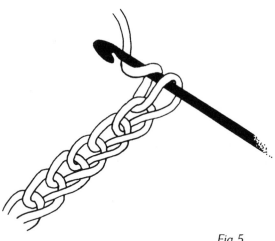

Fig 5

Design 1: Reversible edge-to-edge waistcoat in textured knop yarn (page 60)

Repeat this movement until it becomes quite rhythmical and automatic and continue until the chain is regular and smooth. Run the first finger and thumb along the chain and notice that the front side is smooth and the back is ridged. Always work into the front of the chain and do not allow it to twist.

If your chain stitches are tight use a larger size hook, returning to the original size after the chains have been worked.

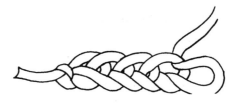

FRONT CHAIN

Fig 6

BACK CHAIN

Fig 7

Design 2: Collared bomber jacket with snug welts worked in a wide variety of Tunisian stitches (page 62)

TUNISIAN STITCHES

As many of the stitches illustrated in books today are 'modern inventions' the names may vary from one publication to another. The abbreviations are given as each stitch is described and American terms are given in brackets.

Tunisian Simple (Afghan Stitch) Ts

Make a chain the desired length.
Row 1 Insert hook into 2nd ch, yrh (yo) and pull through. Retain this lp on hook. *Insert hook into 3rd ch, yrh (yo) and pull through retaining lp on hook. Repeat from * into every ch. (Note that the hook is inserted into the top of the chain stitch and not the bottom as in ordinary crochet.)

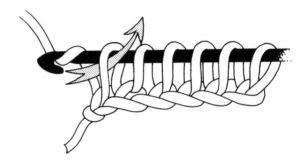

Fig 9

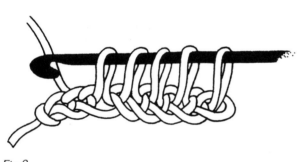

Fig 8

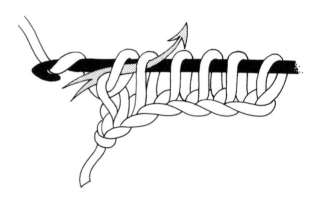

Fig 10

Row 2 *(return row)* yrh (yo) and pull through 1lp. *yrh (yo) and pull through 2lps. Repeat from * to end of row until 1lp is left on hook. The lp left on hook is the first st of next row. It is most important to pull through one stitch only at the beginning of the return row, otherwise the fabric will warp. When working it is very easy to miss this last stitch – if this happens the fabric will not be straight and the number of stitches will decrease. (This row and every alternate row is worked in this way with the exception of a few lacy stitches.)

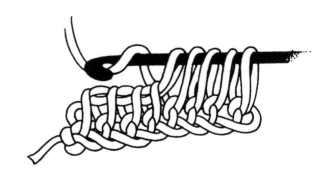

Fig 11

Row 3 Insert hook into 2nd vertical lp, yrh (yo) and pull through retaining lp on hook. Repeat to end of row.
Rows 2 and 3 form pattern
Practise this stitch until you are quite familiar with it and then try mixing colours. (See colour samples on pages 46 and 47.)

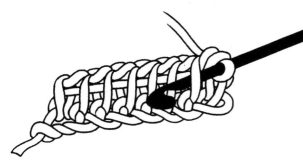

Fig 12

1   When you have reached the left-hand edge of the work take a new colour and tie the end with a single knot on to the thread you have been working with. Work the return row in the usual manner. This makes a coloured chain stitch encased in vertical loops.
2   Work one row of Ts.
3   Work the return row in the original colour.
4   Work Ts in the original colour.
Working in this way creates a fabric which looks as if it is woven. Changing the colour at the right-hand edge will make a solid stripe. Make sure that the edges are straight. If they are not have you missed the end stitch? Check your number of stitches each row until you are quite confident that you can work without missing that last stitch.

Variations
Use three colours and work one row of each colour.
Use four colours and work two rows of each colour.

This simple technique can be used to achieve some quite complicated effects. You now have the skills to do anything which is made from a square or an oblong without shaping; bags, belts, rugs, waistcoats etc. Made up in a plain colour, it can be used as an embroidery canvas for a cushion (see design 12). This stitch makes a fabric which can be cut, so it can be used for garments made by the cut-and-sew method (see design 7).

More Stitches

Now you can do Tunisian Crochet (Afghan Stitch) and it is just a question of learning variations on this stitch to give many other patterns and textures. Some of the stitches tend to warp. This is not always apparent on a small sample and in a garment such as a jumper with few openings the crochet edgings will be sufficient to hold the shape, but front openings will always twist if you have made it in a stitch which warps. Be sure that you know how a stitch makes up before you attempt a larger garment in it.

Tunisian Stocking Stitch Tss

This stitch is worked in the same way as Tunisian simple except for the position of the hook.
Row 1 Insert hook into the centre of the 2nd vertical lp and underneath the chain yrh (yo), and pull through. Continue to the end of the row.
Row 2 (*return row*) Work in the usual way. This stitch makes a firm non-elastic fabric which looks exactly like stocking stitch in knitting but is much firmer. Use a hook two sizes larger than you would for ordinary crochet to avoid a hard fabric.
When you have mastered the stitch try making stripes by changing the colour at the right side of the work.

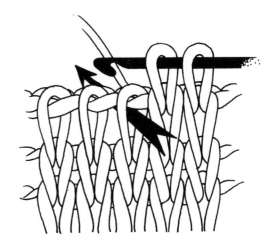

Fig 13

Tunisian Purl Tp

Work Row 1 and return row as for Tunisian simple (Afghan Stitch).
Row 3 Miss 1st vertical thread, *bring yarn to front, insert hook from right to left under 2nd vertical lp. Pass yarn across front of stitch and up behind hook, yrh (yo) and pull through. Repeat from * into every stitch.

Fig 14

Tunisian Stitch Double Td

This stitch is just the Tunisian simple with an extra ch on the top of each stitch. It does need 1ch as a turning chain at the beginning of each alternate row.

Row 1 1ch *insert the hook from right to left under the vertical thread of the previous row, yrh (yo) draw through lp, yrh (yo) draw through lp. Repeat from * leaving all loops on hook.

Row 2 Return row worked in the usual manner.

Variations

Mix this stitch with rows of Tunisian simple. It is a good stitch to use for textured yarn as it brings the yarn to the front of the work and makes any loops more prominent.

Plain Tunisian Stitch

Make a length of ch and work first 2 rows as Ts.

Row 3 Miss 1st 2 vertical threads, *insert hook from front to back of work between next 2 vertical threads and under ch of previous row, yrh (yo) pull 1lp through. Repeat from * to end of row working last st between next to last st of previous row and end st.

Row 4 Return row.

If rows 3 and 4 only are used this will make a warped fabric. Worked in double knitting (knitting worsted) with ten or so stitches this warping effect can be used to make a braid for edgings or belts (see edging for bolero in design 7 and coloured samples).

Variations

Work every alternate 2 rows with another colour. This gives a dog-tooth check effect.

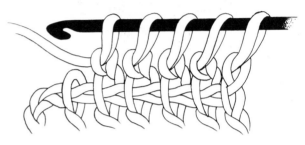

Fig 16

Tunisian Half Treble Tht

Row 1 2ch as turning ch, *yrh (yo). Insert hook behind the vertical bar of the 2nd st, yrh (yo) and pull lp through, yrh (yo) pull through 2lps. Repeat from * to end of row.

Row 2 Return row.

This stitch is useful only to mix with other stitches because it warps badly so that it cannot be used on its own. I have discovered that by putting an extra chain on the top of each stitch the fabric does not warp and forms quite a useful stitch. I have taken the liberty of calling the original half treble and my 'new invention' treble.

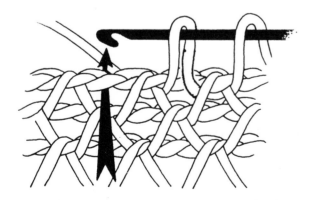

Fig 15

Fig 17

Tunisian Treble Ttr

This stitch has three standing chain which count as the first stitch.

Row 1 yrh (yo), insert hook into 2nd vertical lp, yrh (yo) and pull through (3lps), yrh (yo) and pull through 2lps, yrh (yo) and pull through 1lp, leaving last lp on hook.
Row 2 Return row.

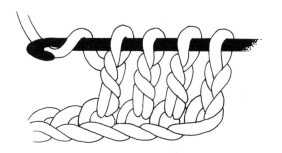

Fig 18

Tunisian Double Treble Tdtr

Works as for Tunisian treble but with 1 extra yrh (yo) and 1 extra tch.

Tunisian Triple Treble Ttr tr

Work as for Tunisian treble but with 2 extra yrh (yo) and 2 extra tch.

Tunisian Bobble Stitch Tb

Make a multiple of 6ch plus 4ch.
Work 1st 2 rows of Ts.

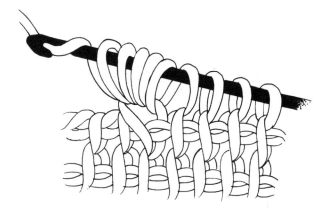

Fig 19

Row 3 1Ts, *1 bobble (made as follows – yrh (yo), insert hook from front to back into next st [yrh (yo) pull through 1lp] 3 times, yrh (yo) and pull through 6lps, yrh (yo) and pull through 1lp), 5Ts. Repeat from * working 1 bobble into 2nd to last st.
Row 4 to 8 Ts.
Row 9 4Ts, *1 bobble into next st, 5Ts. Repeat from * to end of row ending with 1Ts.
Row 10 Return row.

Tunisian Rib Stitch

Make a length of ch and work 2 rows Ts.
Row 3 Miss 1st 5 vertical threads (2½st), *yrh (yo), insert hook from front to back into next st, yrh (yo), pull through, miss next 4 vertical threads, yrh (yo), insert hook into next st and pull through. Repeat from * to end of row.
Row 4 Return row.
Rows 3 and 4 form pattern
It is advisable to check number of stitches every other row until the working becomes automatic.

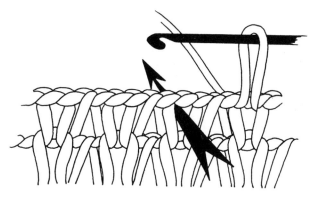

Fig 20

Tunisian Slash Stitch

Make a multiple of 4ch plus 3ch.
Rows 1 to 8 Ts.
Row 9 Change colour, *insert hook from front to back under the ch of previous Ts row, yrh (yo), pull through, yrh (yo), pull through 1lp, repeat from * working 1st 4 rows down, 1st 6 rows down, 1st under the top ch.
Row 10 Return row.
Rows 3 to 10 form pattern repeat

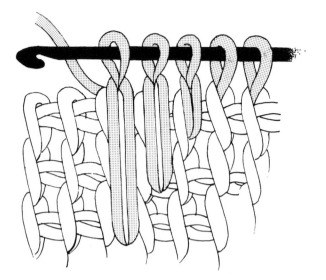

Fig 21

Tunisian Raised Treble Front TRtrF

Rows 1 to 4 Work in Ttr, with corresponding return rows.

Row 5 3ch,* yrh (yo), place hook under the bar of the treble of the previous row, yrh (yo) and pull through, yrh (yo) pull through 2lps, yrh (yo) pull through 1lp and leave on hook. Repeat from * to the end of the row.

Row 6 Return row.

Rows 5 and 6 form pattern

Various textures can be made by alternating the stitch with Ts. Experiment with this stitch and see how many different patterns you can make.

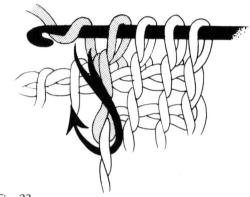

Fig 23

Tunisian Dropped Treble Tdp tr (two colours)

Work 2 rows of Ts and the corresponding return rows (4 rows in all) in colour A.

Row 5 Using colour B miss 1st vertical thread, *1Ttr into 2nd vertical lp of the last row but one, 1Ts into next st. Repeat from * to end of the row.

Row 6 Return row.

Row 7 Using colour A work *1Ts over Ttr of Row 5 and 1Tr over Ts of the Row 5. Repeat from * to end of the row.

Row 8 Return row.

Rows 5 to 8 form pattern

Tunisian Raised Treble Back TRtrB

Rows 1 to 4 Work in Ttr with corresponding return rows.

Row 5 3ch, *yrh (yo), from the back of the work, place hook into the 1st sp in front of the bar of the 2nd st and through the 2nd sp out to the back, yrh (yo) and pull through 2lp, yrh (yo) and pull through 1lp, leave on hook. Repeat from * to the end of the row.

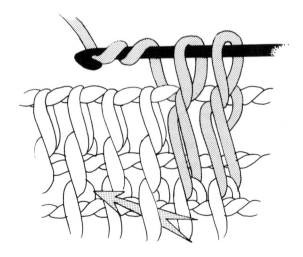

Fig 22

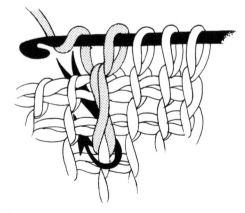

Fig 24

Row 6 Return row.
Rows 5 and 6 form pattern
Think of Tunisian raised treble front and raised treble back as knit and purl stitches in knitting and try out rib and basket stitch patterns. The textured fabric you make will be quite different from knitting but very attractive, especially if two or three colours are used (see colour samples on pages 46 and 47).

Tunisian Raised Double Treble Rdtr

Yrh (yo) twice, place the hook under the stem of the treble and pull through twice. Yrh (yo) pull through once leaving lp on the hook.

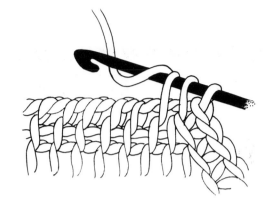

Fig 25

The sixteen basic stitches described can be mixed and matched with random coloured yarns to create many different patterns and fabrics (see stitch samples on pages 46 and 47).

Increasing and Decreasing

This is worked in the same way as in normal crochet (see Appendix 1). As the last stitch is retained on the hook the shaping has to be on the 2nd and 3rd stitches.
To decrease: Put the hook through the second and third stitches and work together. At the end of the row work two stitches together before the last stitch.
To increase: Work an extra stitch in the top of the chain between two stitches.
To decrease a number of stitches: At the beginning of the row slip stitch along the number of stitches to be decreased, then work the turning chain if necessary and continue along the row. At the end of the row slip stitch the number of stitches to be decreased. Break off yarn and rejoin at the last working stitch.
To increase a number of stitches: At the beginning of the row make a chain the number of extra stitches required minus one and add the turning chain. Work along the row. At the end of the row, with a spare piece of yarn, attach a chain of the required number of extra stitches and work along the row.

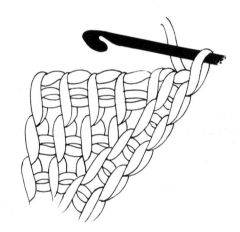

Fig 26

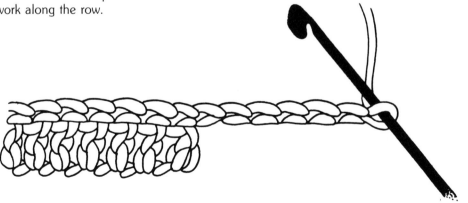

Fig 27

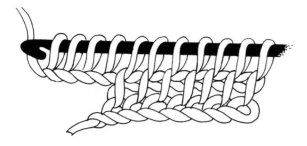

Fig 28

Casting Off (Binding Off)

In Tunisian Crochet it is necessary to 'cast off' (bind off) to give a firm edge for sewing up or to prevent the work curling up. This can be done simply by working one row of slip stitch or double crochet in the usual way on the vertical loop.

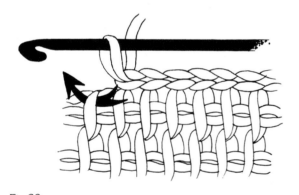

Fig 29

Tunisian Crochet as a Fabric

Tunisian Crochet can be used as a fabric for coats and jackets. Use a dressmaking pattern which has no darts. The fabric is so firm it will not run or ladder. Machine together with the stitch used for stretch fabrics with a very narrow seam allowance. Neaten the seams with zigzag or overlocking stitches. A woven braid as sold in haberdashery shops makes an attractive binding for the edges.

Colour in Tunisian Crochet

Two rows of a second colour will give a stripe if the colour is changed at the right side edge, or if the new colour is introduced at the left side an unusual woven effect is obtained. Experiment with stitches and colours. Work two rows of a number of colours changing the new colour at the beginning of the return row on the left.

Try any of the following:

1   One row of Tunisian treble and one row of Tunisian double crochet using two colours and changing the colour on the left.
2   One row of Tunisian treble and two rows of Tunisian double crochet. Use four colours. This will give a very attractive weave with the wide Tunisian treble stripe a different colour every time.
3   Mix the stitches and work every row a different stitch.
4   Mix the stitches and colours changing the colours on the left and working two rows of every colour.
5   Use different stitches together to make a textured fabric — for example, 2 purl, 2 stocking stitch or 2 dropped trebles and 2 purl.

These are modern interpretations of the old craft and there is no limit to the experimenting you can do. Some stitches you will like more than others but whatever you make it will be exclusive.

TUNISIAN CROCHET WITH A DOUBLE-ENDED HOOK

A double-ended hook looks just like two crochet hooks joined end to end. They are produced in France and America (see Appendix for British suppliers), but as yet I have not seen any pattern or stitches using them.

It is possible to make a double-ended hook with a thin piece of dowelling and a sharp knife or, even better, a fine file and sand paper. Wooden knitting needles can also be reshaped.

The Basic Method (two colours)

1   With colour A make a chain in the usual way and work 1 row Ts.
2   Turn the work and push to the other end of the hook, join on colour B and work the return row.
3   Work 1 row Ts in colour B.
4   Turn the work and push the stitches along to the end of the row and pick up colour A to work the return row.
Continue in this manner until the sample is long enough to show the effect of the double-sided fabric it creates. Working the same method with Tunisian treble and with Tunisian purl will give a thick firm fabric which is like the wrong side of stocking stitch knitting on both sides.

Experiment with different stitches and make up your own patterns (see samples on pages 46 and 47).

Using a double-ended hook in this way makes a very firm fabric which does not roll up, 'curl' or warp. It is very thick and so not suitable for jumpers, but very good for jackets and warmer garments. A thinner fabric for jumpers can be obtained by using Tunisian treble either on its own or mixed with other stitches. Try using several different stitches with contrasting colours and see effects you can create. Remember to write down the stitches used as you work because it is very difficult to work out how an effect was obtained when the sample is finished.

When making garments it is a good idea to work both sleeves and both yokes at the same time to make sure that they match, unless, of course, you like the completely random effect popular in some modern fashions. Yarns of different texture and thickness can be used in the garment provided you do only two rows ('there and back') of any particular yarn. This is an excellent way of using up your odd ends of yarn and the whole effect can be pulled together by working the ribs and edgings in a plain colour (see design 2).

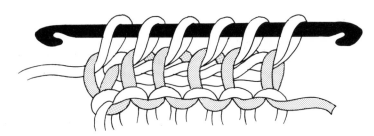

Fig 30

TUNISIAN PATTERNS WITH COLOUR AND STITCH

Illustrated in colour on pages 46 and 47

Colours can be introduced in many different ways, from whole blocks of colour to single rows. The colour can be used from right to left by joining on at the beginning of the row, or from left to right by joining on at the beginning of the return row. Experiment with different colours and different textures of yarn and you will be surprised by the different effects and textures you can obtain in a very easy way. Try some of the following samples putting unusual colours together.

1&3 page 46 2 Colours

20ch. Col A.
Row 1 Col A. Ts.
Row 2 Col B. Return row.
Row 3 Col B. Ts.
Row 4 Col A. Return Row.
These 4 rows form the pattern. The two samples demonstrate different effects from using different yarns.

2 page 46 3 Colours and 3 Stitches

20ch. Col A.
Row 1 Ttr.
Row 2 Col B. Return row.
Row 3 Ts.
Row 4 Col C. Return row.
Row 5 Tp.
Row 6 Col A. Return row.
Repeat this order of stitch and colour.

4 page 46 3 Colours and 4 Stitch Rows

20ch. Col A.
Row 1 Ttr.
Row 2 Col B. Return row.
Row 3 Ts.
Row 4 Col C. Return row.
Row 5 Tp.
Row 6 Col A. Return row.
Row 7 Tp.
Row 8 Col B. Return row.
Continue working with this stitch order and colour sequence.

5 page 46 Tunisian Simple in 2 Colours

20ch. Col A.
Row 1 Ts.
Row 2 Return row.
Row 3 Attach Col B. Work Tunisian Simple (page 21).
Row 4 Return row.
Row 5 Ts in Col A.
Continue working Tunisian Simple and the return row, changing colour every 2 rows.

6 page 46 Tunisian Simple Worked with a Double-ended Hook

20ch. Col A.
Row 1 Ts. Turn work at end of row.
Row 2 Attach Col B and work return row.
Row 3 Tp. Turn work at end of row.
Row 4 Attach Col A and work return row.
These 4 rows form the pattern.

7 page 46 Tunisian Purl Worked with a Double-ended Hook

20ch. Col A.
Row 1 Ts. Turn work at end of row.
Row 2 Attach Col B and work return row.
Row 3 Tp. Turn work at end of row.
Row 4 Attach Col A and work return row.
Rows 3 and 4 form the pattern. Turn work and change colour at the beginning of every return row.

8 page 46 Tunisian Treble Worked with a Double-ended Hook

20ch. Col A.
Row 1 Ttr. Turn work at end of row.
Row 2 Attach Col B and work return row.
Row 3 Ttr. Turn work at end of row.
Row 4 Attach Col A and work return row.
These 4 rows form the pattern.

1 page 47 Waves – 2 Colours

20ch. Col A.
Row 1 Ts.
Row 2 Return row.
Row 3 Col B. *2Ts, 2Thtr, 2Ttr, 2Thtr.
Repeat from * to the end of the row.
Row 4 Return row.
Row 5 Col A. Ts.
Row 6 Return row.
Row 7 Col B. *2Ttr, 2Thtr, 2Ts.
Repeat from * to the end of the row.
Row 8 Return row.
Rows 1 to 8 form the pattern.

2 page 47 Treble and Simple – 2 Colours

20ch. Col A.
Row 1 Col A. Ts.
Row 2 Col B. Return row.
Row 3 Ttr.
Row 4 Col A. Return row.
These 4 rows form the pattern.

3 page 47 Random Stitches and Random Colours Worked with a Double-ended Tunisian Hook

Select a variety of yarns, different colours, different textures. Always turn the work and attach a new yarn at the beginning of the return row.
Use Ttr, Ts, Tp and any other stitches you care to add, in any order. Use whichever side of the finished fabric you prefer as the right side.

4 page 47 Random Stitches and Random Colours Worked with a Single-ended Tunisian Hook

Select a variety of yarns in different colours and textures. Change the colour before the return row and use the yarn for 2 rows only.
Use Ttr, Tp, Ts, 3Tp and 1 dropped Ttr, T puff st and 3 Ts, and any other stitches you care to try, worked in any order.

5 page 47 Tunisian Treble Worked with a Double-ended Hook

Instructions as for No 8 on page 28, but giving a different effect as bouclé yarn has been used.

6 page 47 3 Colours

20ch. Col A.
Row 1 Col A. Ts.
Row 2 Col B. Return row.
Row 3 Col C. Ts.
Row 4 Col A. Return row.
Continue with 3 colours and one stitch.

7 page 47 Tunisian Plain in 2 Colours

20ch. Col A.
Row 1 Ts.
Row 2 Return row.
Row 3 Col B. Place hook under ch and between first and second st, yrh (yo) and pull through. Repeat to the end of the row.
Row 4 Return row.
Row 5 Col A. Place hook under ch and between second and third st, yrh (yo) and pull through. Repeat to the end of the row.
Row 6 Return row.
Rows 3 to 6 form the pattern.

8 page 47 Coloured Square – 2 Colours

20ch. Col A.
Row 1 Pick up 3lps in Col A and 3lps in Col B.
Row 2 Return row. Work 3lps in Col A and 3lps in Col B. Continue working in Ts with 3lps of each colour for 6 complete rows. Work over and under lps of colour at the back.
There are other ways of using colour. Let the colour and texture of the yarn make the pattern for you. Use three different stitches, for example 1 row of Ts, 1 row of Tp and 1 row of Ttr and 4 colours in a regular order as in Design 10.
In Designs 2 and 9, odd wools are used with many different stitches. This is an exciting way to use colour and stitches because you cannot predict exactly how the design is going to turn out or indeed which is the right side of the fabric.

29

TEXTURED TUNISIAN STITCHES

A wide variety of interesting textures can be achieved by using various stitches, examples of which are shown here. Attractive garments can be made by using different stitches in the same design, perhaps by having the yoke and shoulders in an alternative texture to the rest, or sleeves in a contrasting stitch to the main body area.

1 20ch.

Row 1 Ts.
Row 2 Return row.
Row 3 *1Tp, 1Ts, repeat from * to the end of the row.
Row 4 Return row.
Rows 3 and 4 make the pattern.

2 20ch.

Instructions as for stitch 1 until the 4th row has been worked.
Row 5 *1Ts, 1Tp, repeat from * to the end of the row.
Row 6 Return row.
Rows 3 to 6 form the pattern.

3 20ch.

Work as for stitch 1 but work 2Tp and 2Ts which makes a wider rib.

4 20ch.

Work 1 row of Ts and the return row.
Row 3 Place the hook through the chain between the stitches, yrh (yo) and pull through. Repeat to the end of the row.
Row 4 Return row.
Row 5 Miss the first ch between the st but work the rest of the row as Row 3. Work 1 st into the last loop of the row.
Row 6 Return row.
Rows 3 to 6 form the pattern.

5 20ch.

Row 1 Ts.
Row 2 Return row.
Row 3 *Insert the hook under the ch to the right of the 2nd st, yrh (yo) and pull through, insert hook under the ch to the left of the 2nd st, pull through and draw lp through the 2 lps on the hook. Repeat from * for every st.
Row 4 Return row.
Row 3 and 4 make the pattern.

6 20ch.

Row 1 Ts.
Row 2 Return row.
Row 3 1Ts, *1Ts, work 4ch on the top of the st, place the hook into the horizontal lp at the base of the ch, yrh (yo) and draw through 2lps on the hook, 2Ts. Repeat from * to the end of the row.
Row 4 Return row.
Row 5 1Ts, *3Ts, work 1lp as described in row 3. Repeat from * to the end of the row.
Row 6 Return row.
Rows 3 to 6 form the pattern.

Textured Tunisian stitches

BROOMSTICK CROCHET

BROOMSTICK CROCHET

The origins of Broomstick Crochet, or Witchcraft Lace as it is sometimes called, are obscure. The Victoria and Albert Museum in London and the American Museum at Bath have no record or sample of it, yet the Americans claim it as theirs because there is evidence that the early settlers used it as a quick way of making blankets. One can imagine women on the move in their covered waggons using the tools they had to hand, namely a rod or broomstick and a crochet hook, to convert their spare yarn into blankets to keep their families warm. In America, Canada and Australia it is still practised as a traditional craft and is demonstrated in their rural life museums. Many attractive patterns are available in America and it is sometimes called 'Jiffy Lace' because the work grows very quickly.

In Sweden it is called Lattice Loop. It was a peasant craft which probably originated in Europe, and the technique would have been passed on from mother to daughter without any records being kept. It was a craft born of necessity and would only have been practised by poor working women. Odds and ends of handspun yarn would have been used and the finished results warm rather than beautiful. The blankets and shawls would have had constant wear and therefore would not have been treasured as heirlooms. Thus, as with all textile crafts, lack of evidence means that the history is conjecture rather than fact.

Equipment

The crochet hook should be a suitable size for the yarn being used. For example, use a 7.00mm (K) or 8.00mm (11 wood) hook for thick chunky (bulky) yarns and a 3.00mm (C) or 4.00mm (F) hook for finer yarns and cottons.

A very large knitting needle 25mm (1in) in diameter can be used as a 'broomstick', a piece of dowelling from a handicraft shop about 40cm (16in) long can be sanded, polished and sharpened to a point like a pencil, or the end can be sawn off an actual broomstick. A wooden draught or a toy wheel can be tacked or stuck to the end. For finer work with thin yarn or cotton use a finer needle.

Working Method

The principle of Broomstick Crochet is to make loops of a regular size by placing them on to the broomstick and

Design 3: Chunky jacket in natural-dyed pure wool (page 64)

34

to remove them in regular groups with double (single) crochet. The thickness of the finished fabric is decided by the number of loops grouped together. The number of double-crochet stitches in the top of the group is the same as the number of loops, eg five loops are taken off with five double (single) crochet. A warm blanket needs four or five loops together but a floaty evening stole requires only two loops together. There are several ways of putting the loops on to the broomstick and taking them off, and there is no right or wrong way as long as the finished work is pleasing and with a good tension. Each different method produces a slightly different effect. I have given the details of the method I teach first because most people find it the easiest.

Yarn and Colour

Most yarns which are suitable for crochet are suitable for Broomstick with the exception of some mohair yarns which do not slip very easily and so are difficult to use. As there is little variation of stitch it is quite a good idea to use colour for added interest. While experimenting with different ideas you could make the samples of a regular size so they can be joined together to make a scarf or blanket.

When you have become really proficient perhaps you would like to try a blanket on a real broomstick. You will need a chair without arm rests and plenty of space to manoeuvre. Use your odd wools and make every row a different colour (see design 25). Maybe your blanket will become a family heirloom!

Designing with Broomstick Crochet

Broomstick Crochet needs the addition of ordinary crochet or knitting to make the edgings, welts, cuffs, etc. It can be quite a good idea to make only part of the garment in Broomstick. For instance, use Broomstick for the main part of the garment and plain crochet for the sleeves. Alternatively, an evening jumper in a lurex and mohair yarn could have full Broomstick Crochet sleeves. The scalloped edging of Broomstick Crochet often needs no additional edge and it is also possible to use one row of Broomstick as the edging for crochet or knitting.

Design 4: Woven-look jacket in undyed Welsh wool (page 66)
Design 11: Cushion cover worked with a double-ended hook to produce a reversible fabric (page 80)
Design 24: Circular cushion worked in Broomstick Crochet in undyed wool (page 100)

To Work a Sample in the Basic Stitch

1   Use a thick yarn and large hook and make 25ch.
2   Hold broomstick under left arm. (Some people find it more comfortable to hold it between the knees.)
3   Place lp from last ch over broomstick.
4   Insert hook into 2nd ch.
5   Draw a lp through and place it over broomstick.
6   Continue making a lp into every ch (25st). Do not turn.
7   Insert hook into 1st 5lps. yrh (yo) and pull through centre of group. yrh (yo) and pull through the lp making a ch. (This chain is only worked on the 1st group.)

8   Work 5dc (sc) into 1st group of 5lps.
9   Insert hook into next 5lps, remove from broomstick and work 5dc (sc).
10   Continue removing lps in groups of 5 to end of row.
11   Place lp from last st on to broomstick.
12   Still working from left to right, insert hook into the back lp of the 2nd st and pull lp up and on to broomstick.
13   Continue pulling up lps from every st to end of row.
14   Remove lps from broomstick as before.
When you are confident the broomstick can be removed at the end of the first row. The loops will remain in place but care must be taken not to twist them the wrong way.

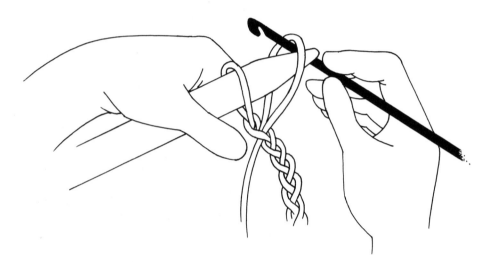

Fig 31

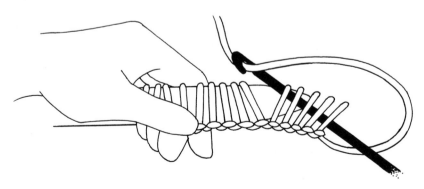

Fig 32

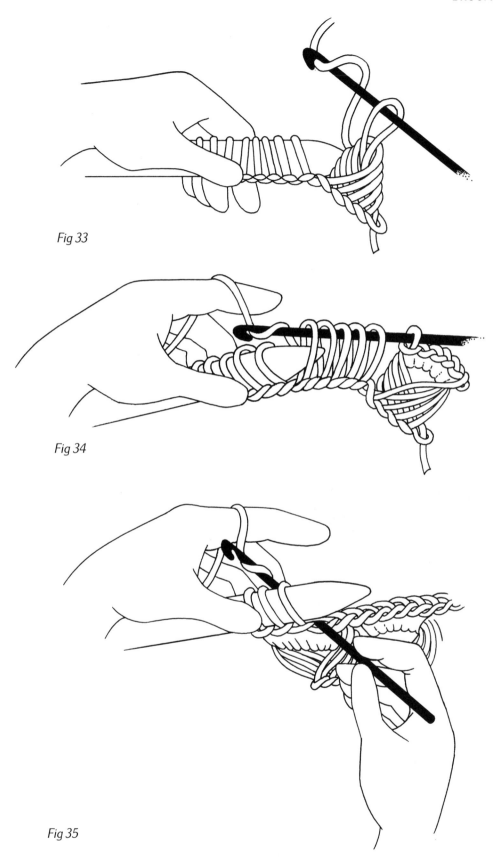

Fig 33

Fig 34

Fig 35

Casting Off (Binding Off)

It is not necessary to make a cast off (bind off) row as in Tunisian Crochet as the double (single) crochet edge is firm enough to sew up or use as a decorative finish. If the edge is to be used as decoration, for example the bottom of a sleeve, you could add another row of double (single) crochet.

Shaping

The looped edge of the work does not lend itself to garments requiring a lot of shaping, for example set-in sleeves, so it is best to choose designs which require straight edges. It is, however, possible to make attractive curves useful for collars or yokes.

Increasing or decreasing is carried out on the double (single) crochet row which means there will be more or less loops on the next row. This will give either a convex or concave curve (see design 23).

To Increase a Number of Stitches

The same principle is used as for ordinary Crochet or Tunisian Crochet. Add a number of chain to the end of the row on the left edge or attach a separate chain to the right edge and pick up the loops working across the row and across the chain at the end.

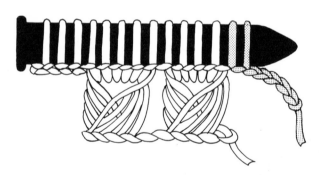

Fig 36

To Decrease a Number of Stitches

Slip stitch over the loops at the beginning of the dc (sc) row the required number to be decreased; work along the row leaving the required number of dc (sc) unworked at the end of the row.

Working 'In the Round'

It is not possible to work Broomstick Crochet in a circle as in ordinary crochet but it is possible to increase so that the work will lie flat and can be sewn up to make a circle. I have not seen this done anywhere else, but I find it works quite successfully and have made circular shawls, cushions and hats in this way (see design 24).
1   6ch. Work 3 broomstick loops into each ch (18lps).
2   Remove the loops 3 at a time with 6dc (sc).
3   Work 1 loop into every dc (sc) (36lps).
4   Remove loops taking 3lps together with 6dc (sc).
Continue increasing this way until the circle is as large as you want it when laid flat. For a hat work three rows of increasing and then continue straight.

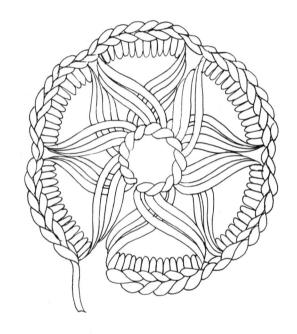

Fig 37

Sewing Up

It is best to make garments with as few seams as possible, but side seams and sleeve seams can be sewn or crocheted together.
To crochet Take 2dc (sc) stitches into the dc (sc) row and make a chain of 4 or 5st across the lp to the next dc (sc) row. This makes a decorative seam and means the garment is reversible. (See Fig 36.)
To sew up Take stitches on the dc (sc) rows, leaving a large loop between the stitches which will lie flat with the other loops.

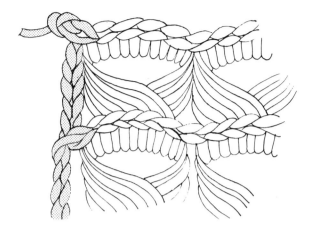

Fig 38

Variations

There are not many variations possible in Broomstick Crochet. Rows of loops can be worked in different colours or rows of loops can be interspaced with rows of double (single) crochet of the same or different colours. It is advisable to use a crochet hook about two sizes smaller for the double (single) crochet rows in order to avoid a fluted effect.

DESIGNING WITH SIMPLE SHAPES

I have tried to include something for everyone among the designs in this book. The garments are all simple classic shapes which never date, and range from an easy Broomstick Crochet collar to a complicated jacket. Some of the designs are described in detail down to the last loop for those of you who have not yet gained the confidence to do your own thing, while others are just sketchy ideas for you to elaborate on and make up your own patterns. For many of the detailed patterns I have also suggested ways in which they can be adapted.

As there are no patterns in the shops for Tunisian and Broomstick Crochet you will soon find you want to design projects yourself. This is not very difficult, it is just a question of experimenting and gaining confidence. Nothing need be wasted, if you do not like your efforts just unpick them and start again. For this reason I advise that you do not use mohair yarn while you are trying an idea out as that is sometimes impossible to unpick.

Collect an assortment of yarns of varying colour and texture by exchanging with friends and buying cheap balls from bins in wool shops. Start by making a square or rectangle. Experiment with stitches and colours which you think look good together. With the woven Tunisian look it is possible to use very unusual combinations of colour and yarn. Make your sample into something, perhaps a bag or cushion, then go on to make a top or over jumper.

Garment Sizes

Modern fashion is often big and baggy which is fine for the young and slim, but not so kind for fuller figures! It also makes a nonsense of much of the sizing of garments as one person's size 12 is another's size 16. For this reason the instructions for garments are not given in sizes but in measurements. The following table shows how to choose the size you require.

Body Measurements	Close Fitting	Standard Fitting	Over sized – Full roomy effect
81cm (32in) Size 10	81–84cm (32–33in)	86cm (34in)	94cm (37in)
86cm (34in) Size 12	86–89cm (34–35in)	91cm (36in)	99cm (39in)
91cm (36in) Size 14	91–94cm (36–37in)	96cm (38in)	104cm (41in)
96cm (38in) Size 16	96–99cm (38–39in)	101cm (40in)	109cm (43in)
101cm (40in) Size 18	101–104cm (40–41in)	106cm (42in)	114cm (45in)
106cm (42in) Size 20	107–109cm (42–43in)	112cm (44in)	120cm (47in)

A Simple Jumper

Cut a paper pattern for the front and back of the jumper. Make it the width you need, by the length you want (see Fig 39). Choose your colour and stitches and crochet two rectangles the size of your pattern. Sew or crochet up the under arm seams leaving the armholes as large as you like them. Sew or crochet the shoulder seams leaving a boat-shaped neck. Add a knitted or crocheted rib at the bottom if you like it shaped (see Fig 38) or leave it loose, perhaps for wear with a belt. It does not matter if you crochet from the top to the bottom, the bottom to the top or from side to side, as long as the fabric you have made is the same size as your paper pattern the garment will fit you.

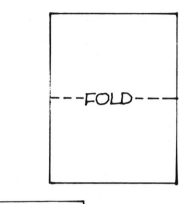

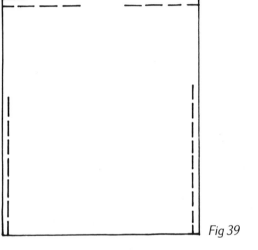

Fig 39

Fig 40

For the Sleeves make two rectangles the length you would like your sleeves by twice the width left for the armholes (probably about 40cm (16in)) and sew in place. Add a ribbed cuff if you like them tight or make them 7cm (3in) longer if you prefer a turned-back cuff (see Fig 39).

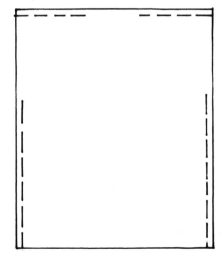

Fig 41

Designing a Waistcoat

Make a paper pattern in the same way as for the jumper and fold in half lengthways. Make two rectangles like scarves which are as wide as the folded pattern and twice as long. Sew or crochet together the folded scarves to make the side seams, leaving an armhole, and sew or crochet together the centre back. Make two 15cm (6in) squares for pockets and add a belt (see Fig 40). Alternatively make the rectangles shorter and add a ribbed waistline. (See design 1.) By now you must be realising how easy it is to use your own ideas for garments. Once you have made something which fits you will soon gain confidence. Look around for other shapes, or copy the ideas from other garments in your wardrobe or from pattern magazines.

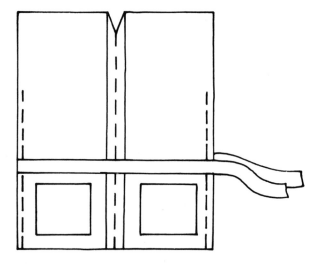

Fig 42

Design 5: Simple-to-make waist-hugging reversible waistcoat (page 68)

(overleaf) A wide variety of samples of Tunisian stitches (instructions given on pages 28 and 29)

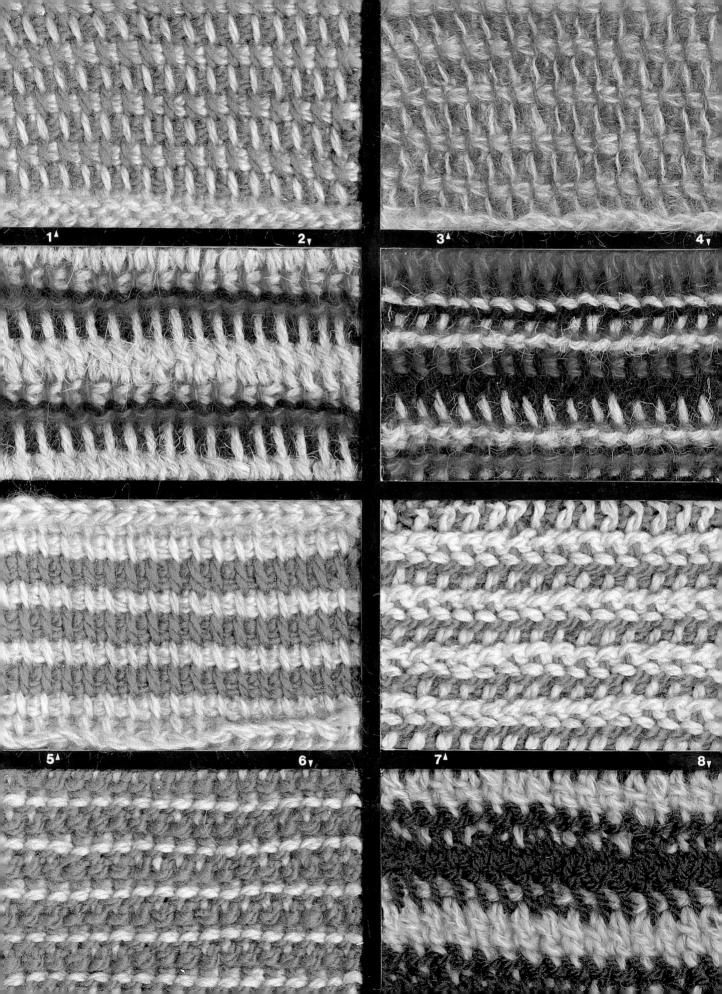

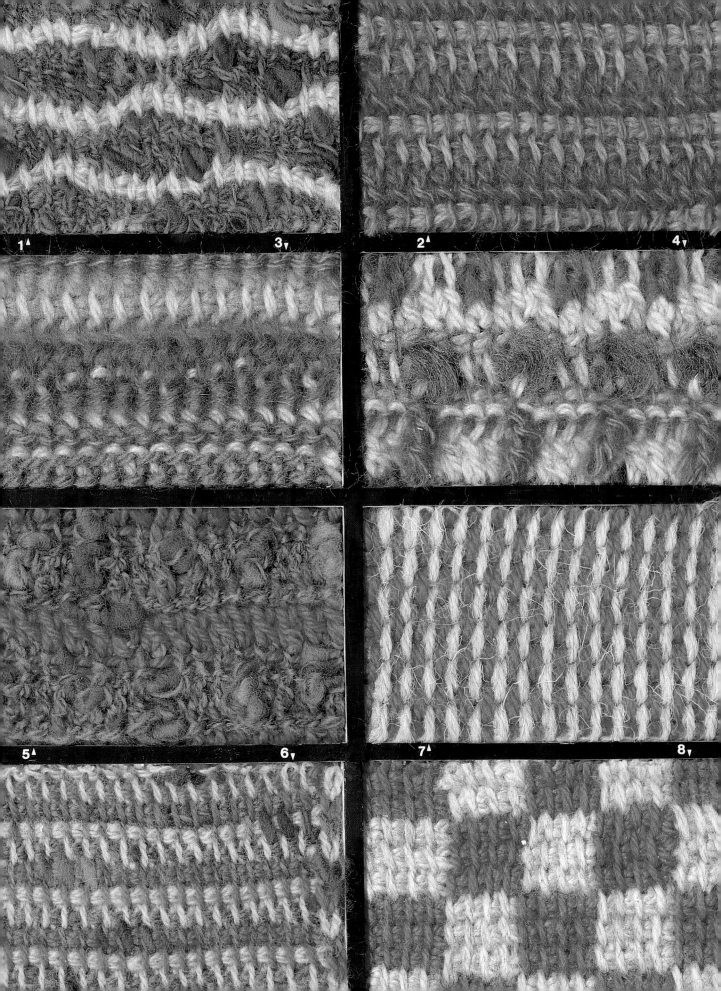

1▲   3▼   2▲   4▼

5▲   6▼   7▲   8▼

Tension (Gauge)

When following a pattern tension is very important – the garment will be a disappointment if it does not fit. Tension is the most difficult thing to cope with in crochet. In knitting most people know that their tension is tight or loose and alter the needle size accordingly, but in crochet everyone's tension is different and indeed your own tension can vary slightly from one week to the next. The tension of the pattern is really the tension of the designer. Before starting to follow a pattern work a tension square as follows:

How to Work a Tension (Gauge) Square

It is tempting to skip making a tension square, but checking the tension is vital to the success of the garment and failure to do this is often the reason for failures with crochet.

1 With the correct yarn and hook make a chain about 20cm (8in) long. Follow the stitch instructions and where the pattern says repeat from * to the end of the row, repeat as many times as your chain will allow. Follow the instructions until you have a square of about 20cm (8in).

2 Cut a piece of cardboard with a window of 10cm (4in) square.

3 Place the square in the centre of the stitch sample and count the number of stitches across the top of the square and the number of rows down the square. Compare this with the details given in the tension section of the pattern.

It is essential to get the number of stitches correct first because the rows are easily adjusted by doing more or less. If there are too many stitches in your sample, try a larger hook. If there are not enough stitches you need a smaller hook. One stitch out in 10cm (4in) could mean anything up to 10cm (4in) difference in the finished width of the garment, so you must get it right before you start. It is also a good idea to recheck your tension when you have completed 5cm (2in) or so of the main garment.

When making my own designs with Tunisian or Broomstick Crochet I have found a 'cheat' which works very well if you find your tension has altered while working. Each row of the work can easily be cut and unpicked on the left hand side and the ends run in. Continue working on the rest of the stitches and nobody will ever know!

Designs 7 and 8: Cut-and-sew bolero and matching A-line skirt (pages 71 and 72)
Design 6: Gloves worked in a Moroccan stitch which the author watched being made in the market place in Marrakesh (page 70)
Design 12: Cushion cover in plain Afghan stitch embroidered with a traditional rose design in cross stitch (page 81)

KNITTED AND CROCHETED EDGINGS

The edgings of a garment are most important and must be worked neatly and accurately. Both sides of the edging strip must match exactly. Left and right fronts must have the same number of stitches whether knitted or crocheted. When picking up the stitches on the main part of the garment it is important to pick up the same part of the stitch every time; failure to do this will result in an untidy finish.

If you find this very difficult, crochet or knit the edgings separately and sew them on, but again care must be taken with every stitch. Oversewing does not always give a good result. I prefer back stitching on the right side on top of the edging, even making a feature of these stitches by using a contrasting colour. Once again the stitches must be accurate and worked into the same part of the loops every time. This method is a good way

of camouflaging an untidy edge on the main garment. When using different yarns and different stitches with Tunisian Crochet the edges are often uneven, so this is a good way of dealing with the problem.

A knitted rib often gives a tighter and smarter finish to the waistline. I find it easier to work the main part of the garment first and then pick up the stitches at the waistline and work down. Cast off loosely in rib.

Use your tension (gauge) square to experiment on. Try various edgings and methods of applying them on this and choose the one which gives the best results. The quality of the end product is far more important than following the instructions of the pattern to the letter.

A variety of knitted and crocheted edgings is given on pages 51 and 52.

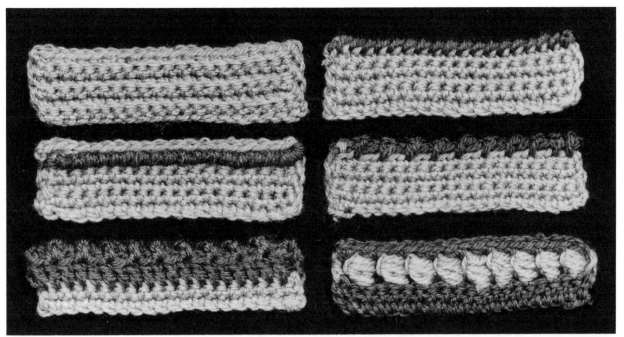

Crochet Edgings

(*top left*) Horizontal ribbing made by working every dc (sc) into the back loop

(*top right*) Crab stitch or reverse dc (sc) making a whipped edge. Work from left to right placing the hook from front to back yrh (yo) and pull through, turning the hook through 180° yrh (yo) and complete the stitch.

(*centre left*) Work crab stitch as above, but work into the front loop only of the row. Work another row from right to left into the back loop of the stitch. This edging does not curl up.

(*centre right*) Work from left to right as in crab stitch, 1tr (dc), 1ch, miss 1st.

(*bottom left*) Double edging with a picot border.

Row 1 tr (dc) into every st.

Row 2 1tr (dc), 1ch, miss 1st.

Row 3 As Row 2.

Fold over and sew in place.

(*bottom right*) A fancy edging for edge-to-edge jackets.

Row 1 2ch, 1htr (hdc)*, yrh (yo), place hook between tch and htr (hdc), repeat from * 3 times, yrh (yo) and pull through. Repeat this st to end of row.

Row 2 Work 2dc (sc) between every 'bobble'.

Shaping Edges

(*top left*) A mitred corner. Work 3dc (sc) into the same stitch on every row.

(*centre left*) A square neckline with a curved edging. On first row of dc (sc) edging, work 1tr (dc) into the corner. On consecutive rows work 2dc (sc) together on either side of the corner stitch.

(*top right*) A rib in dc (sc) worked separately and sewn on to a curve with backstitch.

Knitted Edgings

(*centre right*) Knit 1, purl 1 rib. Cast off in rib.

(*bottom left*) A double thickness edging made by stocking stitch (knit 1 row, purl 1 row) and working 3 purl rows together to form the edge. Sew down at the back.

(*bottom right*) *Knit 2 tog, pass the stitch back on to the left needle. Repeat from * to the end of row. This gives an edge which will stretch.

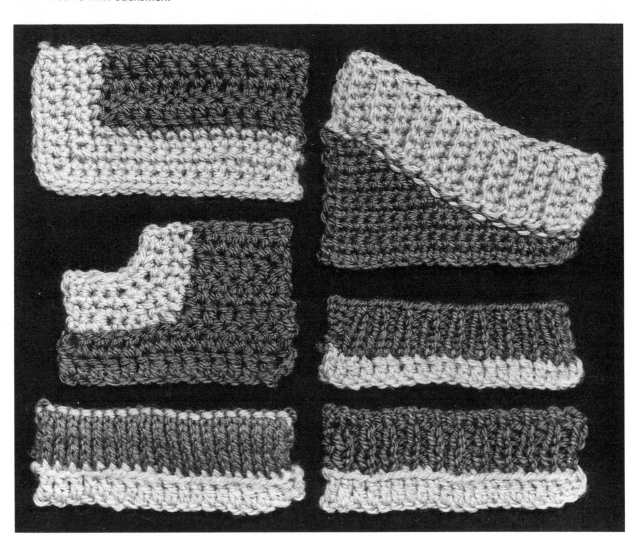

FINISHING OFF GARMENTS

This stage is most important for a well-finished garment. It takes far more time than one would imagine, but as the whole appearance of the garment depends on how well it is sewn up and edged it is time well spent.

Running in Ends

Unpick all the knots and run in ends invisibly on the wrong side of the work. Sometimes a long end can be left for sewing up. When you are using many colours in one design this can be very boring and is probably better tackled as you go along.

Pressing

Always read the instructions given on the wool bands. It is usually unnecessary to press and it does tend to spoil the texture of the fabric you have created. If the garment pieces are out of shape, for instance some Tunisian pieces may be slightly warped, pin the pieces down on a padded base. Check that the side and shoulder seams match up, cover with a damp cloth and leave to dry.

Sewing Up

The edges of Tunisian Crochet are often not very even, especially when several different stitches have been combined. A row of double (single) crochet along the edge will cover up any unevenness and make a firm edge to sew. Experiment with your tension (gauge) square to see which method looks best for the seams with the stitch and colours you have worked.

Oversewing

This is most frequently used but is not always satisfactory when several colours have been worked as the stitches show. With wide stripes of different colours use several needles threaded with the different colours. Sew with the colour of the stripe and slip (skip) along on the wrong side the colours not used. This method sews up the striped fabric without the stitches showing.

Back Stitching

This makes a strong seam and the stitches do not show. It is useful for securing uneven edges, but it does tend to be rather bulky.

Weaving

Place the edges together, matching any pattern, and weave together from side to side on the top making any stitch design match.

Double Crochet

This can be used on the right side as a decoration (see designs 5, 6, 11 and 12) and is very useful for putting sleeves in because it is stretchy and gives with wear. It is also the best way to make up reversible garments (see designs 1 and 5). I prefer to crochet garments together rather than sew because it blends in with the fabric and gives a seam which will stretch.

Slip Stitch

This can be used but only on the wrong side of the garment because the stitch tends to lie one side of the seam and it would look out of place on the right side.

Sewing by Machine

This makes a bulky seam but gives a very smart finish. It is really only to be recommended when using the cut-and-sew method with Tunisian Crochet (see designs 7 and 8). It is very necessary to be absolutely sure of the seam position before sewing because it cannot be unpicked.

Fastenings

Zips

I am not very fond of zips as fastenings because the cotton backing of the zip tends to shrink at a different rate to the yarn of the garment. Also I think zips should be an invisible fastening and this is difficult to achieve satisfactorily.

Buttons

The choice of buttons sold in haberdashery shops can be limited and many of them will do little to enhance your garment. I collect buttons from antique and junk shops, preferring those made from natural materials such as pearl, wood, pottery, etc. Some suppliers of more unusual buttons are listed in Appendix 4. These will probably be more expensive than run-of-the-mill plastic buttons, but the garment you have made will last for years so a little extravagance is excusable. I often use beads instead of buttons with satisfactory results and hand-made buttons using the yarn of the garment also look good.

Caring for your Garments

Do not wear your garment two days in a row and never

FINISHING OFF GARMENTS

use pockets for anything heavier than a handkerchief. Allow the fibres to recover by folding it into shape and storing flat – never hang on a hanger. Shake garments before folding to remove any dirt. Always shake out mohairs or loopy yarns before wearing because they do tend to flatten when folded.

Sometimes wool and woollen mixtures 'pill' where surfaces rub together. If you haven't one of the special brushes for dealing with this, give them a gentle brushing with sticky tape wound round your hand. The little 'balls' can be cut off with scissors or very carefully shaved with a sharp razor.

If you spill something on a garment spot clean immediately with warm water or one of the proprietary cleaners so that the stain does not set. Always mend if necessary before cleaning or washing. Any 'pulls' can be eased through to the back of the garment with a crochet hook. Keep some of the yarn, with a skein band, in case you want to repair or alter the garment.

Washing
Refer to the skein band for the recommended instructions. If you have used a mixture of yarns use the instructions for the most delicate fabric. If in doubt hand wash in warm water with a mild washing powder. Do not rub but squeeze in the water. Rinse several times until all the detergent has gone and give a 15 second spin. Pull into shape and dry flat on a towel. If you feel it necessary to iron the garment use a dry cloth under the iron.

THE DESIGNS

THE DESIGNS

For abbreviations used in designs see page 9.

Design 9: Striking threequarter-length coat made with a double-ended hook (page 73)

MAKING THE PROJECTS

The projects presented in the following pages are intended to be used as a guide. You are encouraged to adapt and design to suit your own needs, not to follow the instructions slavishly to the last stitch. All the garments are made from simple shapes and a tailored fit is not necessary. Ribbing stitches provide the shaping.

Before making anything cut out a paper pattern to your size. Check it against a favourite garment which you know is a good fit. As you work make sure that the fabric you are making is the same size as your pattern — if it is your garment will fit.

After making the pattern try out the stitch by making a tension (gauge) square of about 20cm (8in) square as described on page 49. Decide whether you like the stitch and the colours you have chosen. Now is the time to experiment — this square can be used to try out different kinds of edgings, the neatest way of picking up stitches and the best way to sew or crochet the garment together. Don't be afraid to experiment with stitches, they can always be pulled out and the wool reused, so nothing need be wasted.

Many of the designs include ideas for adapting the pattern for use as something else, so there are many more possible projects than the twenty-six listed if you use your imagination. Most of the garments are suitable for children and the shapes can easily be scaled down to children's sizes. I hope I have included something to interest everyone.

Design 10: Jumper in hand-spun wool with deep inset sleeves (page 78)

Design 1: Reversible Waistcoat made with a Double-ended Hook
Illustrated in colour on page 17

Materials
300gm of Flamme Fine by Scheepjeswol (colour A); 200gm of Aran by Rowan Yarns (colour B); No 7.00mm (K) double-ended Tunisian hook; No 6.00mm (I) crochet hook
Note Alternative yarns may be used. Flamme Fine is a very textured 'nobbly' yarn and the Aran is an easily obtainable contrast

Measurements
Length: 56cm (22in)
Bust: 92cm (36in)
Tension 9st to 10cm (4in)
Rows as measured.

Tension (Gauge)
13st and 16 pattern rows to 10cm (4in).

Stitch Pattern
Make ch with colour A.
Row 1 Ttr into 4th ch from hook. Continue to end. Push work to the end of the hook and turn.
Row 2 Colour B, return row.

Row 3 Ts. Push work to the end of the hook and turn.
Row 4 Colour A, return row.
Rows 1 to 4 form pattern

Adaptations
The waistcoat is made up with an edging which looks almost the same from both sides. The shoulders are crocheted together and so there are no seams. It can be worn with either side as the 'right' side. It can be made longer, patch pockets can be added and a straight sleeve will turn it into a jacket.

Instructions
Back and fronts are worked in one piece to the armholes. With colour A make 123ch.
Row 1 Ttr into 4th ch from hook.
Work in stitch pattern until 38cm (15in) have been completed. To divide work for the yokes work 25st, sl st 10st, work 50st, sl st 10st. Continue in pattern to the end of the row.

Left Front
Continue working on the left front for 13cm (5in). sl st

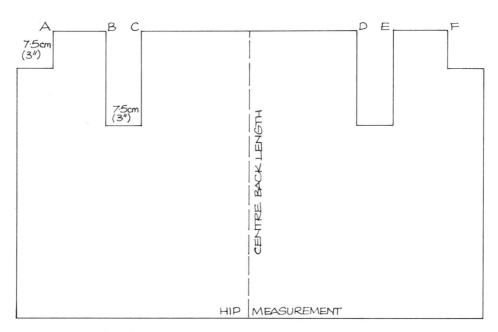

AB and EF = ⅓ of CD

Fig 43

over 8st for the neck edge and continue working on the remaining 17st for another 7cm (3in). Cast off (bind off) by sl st along the row.

Back
Work in stitch and colour pattern on the centre 50st for 20cm (8in). sl st to cast off (bind off).

Right Front
Work in stitch and colour pattern to match the left front.

To Make Up
Place the front shoulders in position on the back and dc (sc) to the back.

Edging
Use crochet hook No 6.00mm (I).
Row 1 Join colour A to centre back of neck and dc (sc) around the neck, the front edges and the bottom finishing at the centre back, working 3dc (sc) into 1st at the corners.

Row 2 Colour B 3ch * 1htr (hdc), yrh (yo) and place hook back round the stem of the htr (hdc), yrh (yo) twice more, yrh (yo) and pull through all the loops. Miss 1st and repeat from *. Work this stitch all round the garment. To mitre the corners work the 'bobbles' into 3 consecutive st. When the round is completed sl st to top of the first standing ch.
Row 3 With colour A work 2dc (sc) into every space between the bobbles. At the end of the round sl st to finish off. Work 3dc (sc) into the corners.

Armhole Edging
Join colour A to the centre of the 10st at the bottom of the armhole and work the stitch to match the front edging.

Finishing Off
Run in all ends. Pull into shape, this stitch does not need any pressing. Wear the garment with the side you like best as the right side.

Design 2: Bomber Jacket with Snug Welts Worked in a Wide Variety of Tunisian Stitches
Illustrated in colour on page 18

Materials
1,200gm of odd yarns including 250gm of one shade for the waistband, cuffs and collar; No 7.00mm (K) Tunisian hook; No 6.00mm (I) crochet hook; 8 buttons.

Measurements
Length: 56cm (22in)
Bust: 97cm (38in)
Back neck to bottom of sleeve: 66cm (26in)

Design Note
This garment will be entirely your own design because you choose the colours, the stitches and the order in which they are worked. Start at the centre back and work to the cuff. If you wish to have both sides matching, as in the garment illustrated, it is a good idea to have two Tunisian hooks and work a few rows at a time on both sides. I find this is much easier than completing one half then repeating all the colours and stitches to make the other side match. On the other hand you can make the whole garment completely random, with no matching sides or sleeves.

Tension (Gauge)
13st to 10cm (4in). Rows as measurements.

Stitch Pattern
Use any of the Tunisian stitches you know in any order you like. The return row will always be the same. Start new colours at the beginning of the return row, changing colour every other row. Run in the ends as you go along to save a mammoth task at the end.

Instructions
Right Back
Make 73ch.
Row 1 Ttr into 4th ch from the hook. Continue to end.
Row 2 Change yarn. Return row. Work 7.5cm (3in) in stitches and colours of your choice. Return to the base chain and pick up stitches into the first row worked. Work 7.5cm (3in) for the left back. Put this on one side.

Right Front
Make 61ch. Work exactly as the back, for 8cm (3in) adding 12ch to the last row for the side of the neck.

Left Front
Work exactly as the right front, attaching 12ch to the left side of the work.

Fronts and Backs Together
Left Side
Work across the front over the 12ch and along the back for 23cm (9in). If you wish to make a larger size add more rows at this point.

Under-arm Shaping
sl st 14st at the beginning of the row and leave 14st at the end of the row. Continue decreasing 2st at each end of every outward row until 50st remain. Work straight for 28cm (11in) or until the sleeve is long enough, allowing 9cm (3½in) to be added for the cuff.

Right Front and Back
Work to match the left front and back.

Cuffs
Make 16ch. Work a strip to match the waistband 20cm (8in) long. Crochet into a circle and dc (sc) to the end of the sleeve.

Collar
Make 32ch. Work a strip to match the waistband 43cm (17in) long. Crochet in dc (sc) all around the neck edge. Place collar around the neck and dc (sc) into position. Work round buttonholes with buttonhole stitch. Sew on buttons.

To Make Up
Run in all ends. Fold the garment along the shoulder line with right sides together and oversew the underarm and side seams.

Waistband
Work 1 row dc (sc) along the bottom edge of the garment to tidy the ends of the Tunisian rows.
Row 1 19ch. Into 2nd ch from hook work 1dc (sc). dc (sc) to the end of the row.
Row 2 dc (sc) into the back lp of the 2nd st. Continue working dc (sc) into the back of the st to the end of the row.
Work a strip 72cm (28in). Attach to the bottom of the jacket with 1 row dc (sc).

Left Front Rib
Pick up and work dc (sc) along the left front and across the waist rib. Work 4 more rows in dc (sc).
Row 5 Working from left to right work crab st (see page 51) into the front lp of the st.

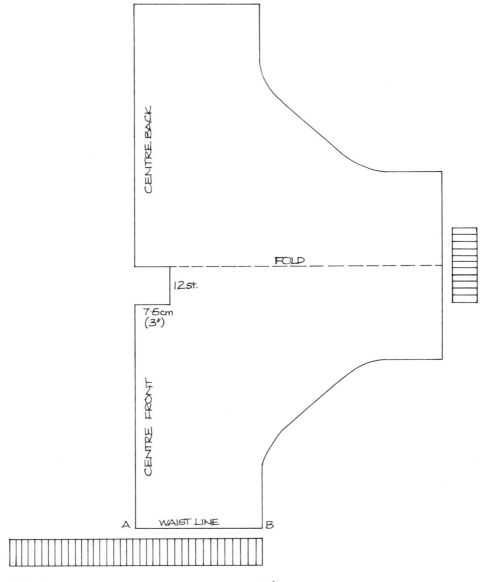

CENTRE BACK

FOLD

12 st.

7·5cm
(3")

CENTRE FRONT

A   WAIST LINE   B

AB = ¼ WAIST MEASUREMENT + 2·5cm (1")

Fig 44

Row 6 Working from right to left work dc (sc) into the back lp of the st behind the crab st. This makes an edging which does not curl.

Right Front Rib
Pick up as for left front
Row 3 Make buttonholes as follows: 2dc (sc), miss 2st 2ch, 9dc (sc). Repeat 8 times. dc (sc) to end of the row.
Row 4 dc (sc).
Rows 5 and 6 Crab st, as for the left front rib.

Design 3: Chunky Jacket in Natural-dyed Pure Wool
Illustrated in colour on page 35

Materials
1,200gm of chunky (bulky) wool; No 8.00mm (11 wood) Tunisian hook; No 7.00mm (K) crochet hook; 8 buttons
Note The wool used for the jacket illustrated was 'rainbow dyed' by Gloria Watson of Manor Farm Cottage, West Stour, Dorset. Naturyarn by Jaegar makes a good alternative, but any chunky (bulky) yarn can be used.

Measurements
Length: 64cm (25in)
Bust: 108cm (42in)
Sleeve: 51cm (20in)

Tension (Gauge)
12st to 10cm (4in). Rows as measurements.

Stitch Pattern
Row 1 Ts.
Row 2 Return row.
Row 3 Ttr.
Row 4 Return row.
These 4 rows are worked throughout but the edgings are in ordinary dc (sc), finished with a crab st. See page 51.

Instructions
The pocket backs are worked first. The back and fronts are worked all in one piece to the armhole.

Pocket Backs (make 2)
On the Tunisian hook make 20ch.
Row 1 Ttr into 4th ch from hook. Ttr to the end of the row.
Row 2 Return row.
Continue in stitch pattern until 2 complete patterns and 1 row of Ts have been worked. Put on one side on another hook.

Back and Fronts
Make 115ch. Work 3 complete stitch patterns.

To Make Pockets
Row 1 6st in pattern. sl st across 17st, pattern 66st. sl st 17st, pattern 6st.
Row 2 Return row. Pin the pocket backs already worked into position behind the sl st of the previous row. Work the return row across the garment and the pocket backs. The pockets can be sewn down when the garment is finished.
Continue working until the garment measures 35cm

(14in). For a longer coat more rows can be added at this point.

Dividing for the Yokes
Work 23st in pattern. sl st across 10st, work 46st. sl st across 10st finishing with 23st.

Left Front
Continue working on the last 23st for 2st patterns and 1 row of Ttr plus the return row.

To Shape Neck
Work 17st in pattern. sl st across 6st and break off wool. Rejoin wool and work 10cm (4in) in pattern. sl st to cast off (bind off).

Back Yoke
Rejoin wool to the centre 46st and work in pattern until the back yoke is the same length as the left front. sl st to cast off (bind off).

Right Front
Work on the remaining 23st to match the left front and sl st to cast off (bind off).

Sleeves
Worked from the armhole towards the wrist.
Make 51ch. Work in stitch pattern for 10cm (4in). Decrease 1st each end every 4 rows until there are 36st. Work until sleeve measures 42cm (16½in). Decrease for cuff by taking 2st together every other st until there are 24st. sl st to cast off (bind off).

Front and Bottom Edging
Work the edgings before inserting the sleeves. Sew up shoulder seams. Start at the neck edge of the left front. With an ordinary crochet hook dc (sc) down the left front across the bottom and up to the neck of the right side taking 3st into one space to mitre (see page 52) the corner at the bottom of the fronts.

With pins mark the position of the buttonholes. Work a buttonhole by missing 2 or 3st and working 2 or 3ch according to the size required by the buttons. Shaping the mitres at the bottom of the fronts, work a total of 3 rows for the edging.

Collar
With right side of garment facing, join wool to the right side of the neck and work round the neck to the left side taking 1tr (dc) into the corners. Continue in dc (sc) for 6

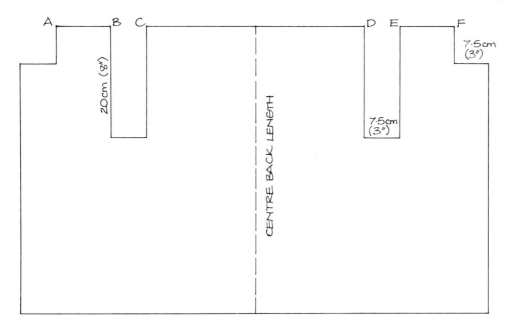

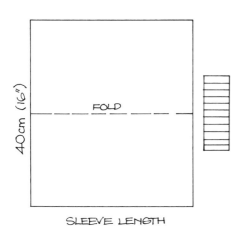

SLEEVE LENGTH

AB and EF = ⅓ of CD

Fig 45

rows. Decrease 1st either side of each corner of the neck on alternate rows.

Corded Edging (see page 51)
Attach wool to the centre of the bottom edge. With right side facing work 1ch and crab st from left to right all the way round the fronts and the collar working 2st into 1 at the mitred corners. sl st the last st to the first ch to make an invisible join.

Sleeves
Wrong sides together, pin the centre of the sleeve head to the shoulder seam. Working with the sleeve facing, dc(sc) from the armhole corner along the sleeve head to the other side. Sew the bottom of the armhole to the side of the sleeve on each side. Turn the garment inside out and sew the sleeve seam from the under arm to the cuff.

Cuffs
Work 6 rounds of dc (sc) finishing each round with a sl st into the turning ch of the previous row, 1ch. Finish with 1 row of crab st to match the front edgings.

Pocket Welts
Sew pocket lining into position. Attach wool to the top of the pocket. Work 3 rows of dc (sc) finishing with 1 row of crab st.

Finishing Off
Sew on buttons. Work buttonholes to prevent stretching. Pull into shape, pressing should not be necessary.

Design 4: a Woven-look Jacket
Illustrated in colour on page 36

Materials

7×100gm balls dark black sheep wool (colour A); 3× 100gm balls natural black sheep wool (colour B); No 7.00mm (K) Tunisian hook; No 6.00mm (I) crochet hook; 6 rosewood buttons

Note The dark wool comes from a flock of Black Welsh Mountain sheep bred in Norfolk. The fleece of these sheep, called Cochddu, was a highly valued product of the medieval woollen industry. The light wool is from other breeds. The wool is very hard wearing, undyed and will last for years (see Appendix 4 for supplier). Any yarn of Aran (fisherman) thickness can be substituted.

Measurements

Length: 61 (66)cm; 24 (26)in
Bust: 102 (112)cm); 40 (44)in
Sleeve: Under arm to wrist 49 (54)cm; 19 (21)in

Tension (Gauge)

16st and 14½ rows to 10cm (4in)

Colour Pattern

The colour is changed on the left for the return row.

Stitch Pattern

The stitch pattern is one row of Tunisian treble and one row of Tunisian simple, both with return rows.
Row 1 Colour A, Ttr.
Row 2 Colour B, return row.
Row 3 Ts.
Row 4 Colour A, return row.

Design Note

The jacket is worked sideways, starting at the centre back and centre front and working to the side seams. The sleeves are also worked sideways. All edgings are in double (single) crochet and have a corded edging of crab stitch.

Left Back

With colour A make 87 (95)ch on the Tunisian hook.
Row 1 yrh (yo), hook into 4th ch and work 1Ttr. Work in this stitch to the end of the chain (84 (92)st).
Row 2 Change to colour B and work the return row.
Row 3 Ts into the 2nd st and to the end of the row.
Row 4 Colour A, return row.
These 2 stitches with the colour change make the pattern throughout.
Continue working in pattern until 7 (8) complete patterns have been worked. To make a larger size add more rows at this stage.

To Shape Armhole

sl st over 32 (34)st. Work 2 more complete patterns. sl st to cast off (bind off).

Right Back

Using colour A and with right side of work facing, attach wool to base of 1st st. 3ch, Ttr into every st. Continue in pattern until 7 (8) complete patterns have been worked. Break off colour B.

To Shape Armhole

3ch, Ttr 51 (57). Rejoin colour B and work return row. Work in pattern to match the other side.

Right Front

With colour A make 75 (83)ch. Work 2 complete pattern rows.
Row 9 Ttr.
Row 10 Colour B, return row, 12ch.
Row 11 12Ts into ch. Ts to end of row.
Row 12 Colour A, return row.
Rows 13 to 20 (13 to 24) Work in pattern.
Row 21 (25) Sl st over 32 (34)st. 3ch, Ttr to end of row.
Row 22 (26) Colour B, return row.
Row 23 to 28 (27 to 32) Continue in pattern. sl st along row to cast off.

Left Front

With colour A make 75 (83)ch. Work 2 complete pattern rows.
Row 9 Ttr.
Row 10 Return row.
Row 11 With colour B attach 12ch to end of row. Work across the row and along the additional ch.
Row 12 Colour A, return row.
Rows 13 to 21 (13 to 25) Continue in pattern.
Row 22 (26) Return row.
Row 23 (27) Colour A, Ttr leaving the last 32 (34)st.
Row 24 (28) Rejoin colour B, return row.
Rows 25 to 29 (29 to 33) Continue in pattern. sl st along row to cast off (bind off). Rejoin colour A and sl st along armhole edge.

Sleeves (make 2, worked sideways)

With colour A make 70 (78)ch. Work in stitch and colour pattern for 14 (16) complete patterns. Work 1 row Ttr. sl st to cast off (bind off).

Patch Pockets (make 2)

With colour A make 25 (27)ch. Work 3 complete stitch and colour patterns.

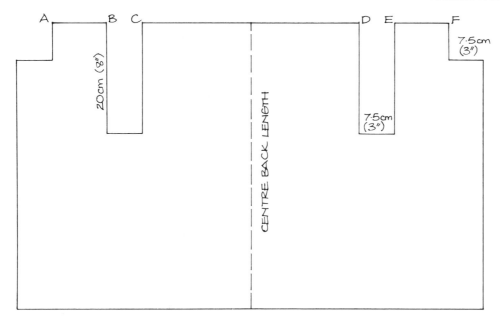

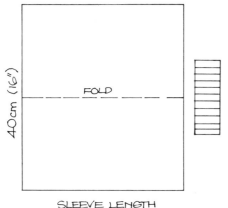

AB and EF = ⅓ of CD

Fig 46

Row 7 Ttr.
Row 8 Colour B, return row.
Join colour A with 7.00mm (K) hook to right edge of work and work 3 rows of dc (sc) followed by 1 row of crab st.

To Make Up

With right sides together, oversew shoulder seams. Find centre of sleeve head and, with wrong sides together, pin sleeve to shoulder seam of jacket. With sleeve facing, crochet sleeve into armhole with 1 row of dc (sc) in colour A. Oversew side of sleeve to bottom armhole edge on front and back. Turn garment inside out and oversew sleeve and side seams. Repeat on the other side.

Cuffs

Pick up 30 (34)st along the bottom of the sleeve. Work 12 rows of dc (sc). Finish off with 1 row of crab st.

Bottom Edge

Work 11 rows of dc (sc) along the bottom edge.

Left Front Edge

Starting at the neck, work 3 rows of dc (sc).

Right Front with Buttonholes

Row 1 Work 70 (78)dc (sc).
Row 2 1ch 4 (5)dc (sc), *miss 3st, 3ch, 9 (10)dc (sc). Repeat from * 5 times, miss 3st, 3ch, 3 (5)dc (sc).
Row 3 1ch, dc (sc) to end of row and finish off.

Collar

With right side of jacket facing, start 2.5cm (1in) from the front edge and work along the neck edge with dc (sc) making 1tr (dc) into the corners of the neck at each side. This will fill in the right angle and make a curve. Work 7 rows of dc (sc) decreasing 2st tog twice at the neck curve on every alternate row.

The Corded Edge

Row 1 Start at the centre of the bottom edge and join on. Work from left to right in crab stitch into the front lp of stitch all round the fronts and collar, increasing 2st into 1 round the corners.
Row 2 dc (sc) into the back lp of stitch.

Finishing Off

Work round buttonholes in buttonhole stitch to prevent stretching. Sew on buttons to match buttonholes. Sew pockets into position.

Design 5: Reversible Waistcoat
Illustrated in colour on page 45

Materials
300gm of Colinette Mohair (colour A); 200gm of space-dyed unplied Colinette wool Point Zero (colour B); Tunisian hook size 7 (K); Crochet hook size 6 (I); 3 2.5cm (1in) buttons.
Note Any mohair and textured yarn can be substituted but particular attention must be paid to keeping the correct tension.

Measurements
Length: 61cm (24in)
Bust: 92–97cm (36–38in)

Tension (Gauge)
12st to 10cm (4in). For this design, measurements are given instead of number of rows.

Stitch Pattern
Row 1 Colour A, Ttr.
Row 2 Return row.
Row 3 Ts.
Row 4 Return row.
Row 5 Colour B, Tp.
Row 6 Return row.
Row 7 Colour A, Ts.
Row 8 Return row.

Rows 1 to 8 form pattern
The two main pieces are worked in this stitch. The edgings are in dc (sc) – ordinary crochet.

Design Note
The garment is made of two long straight strips which are folded in halves and crocheted together to make the side seams and centre back.

Adaptations
The illustrated garment is reversible – the mohair gives a very fluffy effect on the wrong side which may be preferred to the smoother right side. A hip-length waistcoat can be made by leaving off the ribbed waistband and making the two parts of the garment longer by adding more stitches. Patch pockets with horizontal stripes could be added.

Front and Back (make 2)
With colour A make 123ch on the Tunisian hook.
Row 1 1 Ttr into the 4th ch and continue in the stitch pattern until 19cm (7½in) have been worked.
To make a larger size add more rows at this stage.

Right Front Edging
With colour A and the ordinary crochet hook
Row 1 Add 14ch to make extension to waistband. Into 2nd ch work 1dc (sc) and continue in dc (sc) to the end of the row, 1ch.
Row 2 Dc (sc) to end of the row, 1ch.
Row 3 Make buttonholes as follows: 2dc (sc) [3ch, miss (skip) 3st, 6dc (sc)]. Repeat 3 times. Continue in dc (sc) to end of row.
Rows 4 and 5 As Row 2. Finish off.

Front Edging
Use colour A and the ordinary crochet hook.
Row 1 With a spare piece of wool attach 14ch to the left side of the strip. Return to the beginning of the row and work to the end and across the 14ch in dc (sc).
Row 2 Dc (sc).
Row 3 Work across the row to the last 23st and make the 3 3ch buttonholes as on the right side.
Rows 4 and 5 As Row 2.

Side Edgings
Using colour A, attach wool to the bottom row and work 3 rows of dc (sc). Fold strips in halves and dc (sc) the 2 sides together, leaving an armhole of 23cm (9in) unworked.
Finish off.

Centre Back Seam
Place the two centre backs together and crochet together with dc (sc). Finish off 10cm (4in) before half way, leaving a V for the back neck.

Waistband
Attach wool to the waistband extension of 14ch and work in dc (sc) taking each stitch into the back of the stitch on every row. This gives a mock rib. When the strip is 66cm (26in) long attach it to the other waistband extension with dc (sc).

To Make Up
Sew the waistband invisibly to the garment by placing the work flat and taking stitches alternately on the waistband and the main garment.

Button Strip
Make 24ch. Work 4 rows of dc (sc). Sew buttons on to the strip. Work round the buttonholes with buttonhole stitch to prevent them stretching. Decide which side is to be outside and place the button strip accordingly.

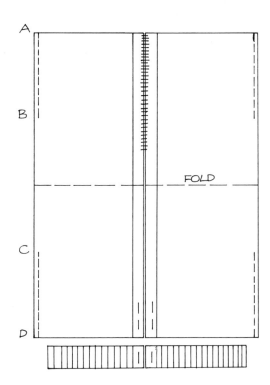

BC = ARMHOLE 40cm (16")
AD = 2 × LENGTH

Fig 47

Design 6: Gloves in a Stitch from Marrakesh
Illustrated in colour on page 48

When I was on holiday I paid a visit to the market place in Marrakesh. This is a fantastic hotchpotch of Berber and Arab life with story tellers, witch doctors, dancers, water carriers and much more. There was a row of Berber women sitting on the floor with their crochet, selling gloves and skull caps they had made. One of them taught me her stitch and I returned the next day to teach her my Tunisian Crochet.

She was holding her wool and hook in the right hand as for knitting. She placed the hook into the back loop of the stitch and worked a slip stitch, working round in a circle. This technique makes a thick, firm fabric which looks like garter stitch in knitting on the wrong side. If it is worked flat the rows are worked from right to left every time and at the end of each row the wool has to be finished off. When I got home I looked the stitch up in the *Encyclopaedia of Needlework* by Thérèse de Dillmont. She calls it Bosnian Crochet, which apparently was used mostly for colourful braids in Victorian times.

Materials
150gm of Aran (fisherman) thickness wool; a few small amounts of contrasting colours for stripes; No 6.00mm (I) crochet hook.
Note The wool used for the gloves illustrated was hand spun.

Tension (Gauge)
17st and 23 rows to 10cm (4in).

Stitch Pattern
Place the hook into the back loop of the st, yrh (yo), pull through and complete a sl st.

Instructions
Right Hand.
Make 35ch. Work 1 row of dc (sc). At the end of the first row join the work into a circle and place a coloured thread to mark the end of a round.
Work stripes as follows: 4 rounds of colour A, 2 rounds of colour B, 1 round colour A, 2 rounds of colour C, 1 round of colour A, 2 rounds of colour C, 2 rounds of colour A, 2 rounds of colour B, 4 rounds of colour A.

To Shape for Thumb
Round 1 At the beginning of the round work 2st into 1, work 2st, 2st into 1, continue to the end of the round.
Round 2 Work in st without shaping.

Continue increasing 2st every other round with 2 extra stitches between the increases each round until 16 rounds have been worked (16 extra st).

To Divide Stitches for Thumb
Miss 16st, 4ch and continue the round. This makes a circle which will be made into the thumb later. Work straight for 8 rounds.

First Finger
Work 6st, 4ch, work 6st from the end of the round. These 16st form the first finger. Continue working this in rounds for 12 rounds. Decrease at the top of the finger by working 2st tog until only 1st is left. Break off wool, thread through the last stitch and sew in the end.

Second Finger
Rejoin the wool to the bottom of the first finger. Pick up 4st, work 4st from the back of the glove, cast on 4st and work 4st from the front of the glove. Work 15 rounds on these st and finish off as for the first finger.

Third Finger
Pick up the stitches as for the second finger and work 12 rounds. Finish off as for the other fingers.

Fourth Finger
Pick up 4st at the bottom of the third finger and work along the rest of the stitches for 10 rounds. Finish off as for the other fingers.

Thumb
Pick up 4st across the palm of the glove and work the rest of the stitches to make the thumb. Work 10 rounds, decreasing 1st on 2 rounds. Shape as for the fingers.

Left Hand
Work as for the right hand until the shaping for the thumb. Increase on the last 4st of the round. Continue shaping as for the right hand.

To Divide Stitches for Thumb
Work the round until the last 16st, 4ch, miss 16st and continue the next round.
Continue shaping the fingers as for the right hand.

Finishing Off
Run in all ends. Work 1 round of dc (sc) into the casting on ch to tidy the bottom of the glove. Press with a cool iron.

Design 7: Cut-and-Sew Bolero
Illustrated in colour on page 48

Materials
700gm Fine Napp yarn used double (colour A).
50gm 3 ply botany wool (colour B for braid); Butterick dressmaking pattern No 3971 (Size 14); No 7.00mm (K) and No 4.00mm (F) Tunisian hooks matching thread for the machine.

Note The wool used for the bolero illustrated came from Rowan Yarns (see Appendix 4). Any 4 ply (sport) or double knitting (knitting worstead) yarn can be substituted.

Measurements
Length: 58cm (23in)
Bust: 91cm (36in)

Stitch Pattern
The main fabric is worked in Tunisian simple (Afghan stitch) and the braid in Tunisian plain.

Adaptations
Any of the firm 'blanket' stitches can be substituted for Tunisian simple (Afghan stitch).

Instructions
With No 7.00mm (K) hook and colour A make three pieces of fabric in Ts large enough to take the pattern pieces of the back and fronts. Press with a damp cloth (this should only be done if the yarn used is 100 per cent wool). Pin the paper pattern on to the fabric and tailor tack the seam positions. Cut out. Stitch all round each piece .25cm (⅛in) from the edge with a straight machine stitch, using matching thread. Tack garment together and adjust fit. Machine shoulder and side seams and press open with a damp cloth. Neaten seams with a widely spaced zigzag stitch.

The Braid
With colour B make 10ch on No 4.00mm (F) hook.
Row 1 Ts.
Row 2 Return row.
Row 3 Place hook under ch and in between 1st and 2nd sts, yrh (yo) and pull through. Repeat to the end of the row.
Row 4 Return row.

Rows 3 and 4 form pattern

Continue in stitch pattern for 5m (5½yd). This forms a narrow braid which slants to the right and looks as if it is 'on the cross'.

Binding the Edges and Armholes
Place the right side of braid to the right side of garment along the seam position and machine into place. Turn the braid over to bind the edge and sew down by hand. Press with a damp cloth to finish.

Design 8: A-line Skirt to Match the Bolero
Illustrated in colour on page 48

Materials

600gm 3 ply botany wool (colour A); 100gm Fine Napp yarn used double (colour B); No 7.00mm (K) Tunisian hook; No 4.00mm (F) crochet hook; 76cm (30in) elastic 2.5cm (1in) wide for the waist.

Note The wool used for the skirt illustrated came from Rowan Yarns (see Appendix 4). Any 4 ply (sport) or double knitting (knitting worstead) yarn can be substituted.

Measurements

Length: 68cm (27in)
Waist: 66cm (26in)
Hips: 97cm (38in)

Stitch Pattern

Row 1 Colour A. 6Ts 15Tht. Ttr to end of row.
Row 2 Return row.
Row 3 65Ts. Tht to end of row.
Row 4 Return row.
Row 5 Ts.
Row 6 Return row.
Row 7 As Row 3.
Row 8 Return row.
Row 9 As Row 1.
Row 10 Return row.
Row 11 Change to colour B. Tp.
Row 12 Return row.

Adaptations

To lengthen garment add more stitches, to shorten deduct stitches. To make the garment larger at the waist work extra panels. Each panel is 4cm (1½in) at the waist and 6cm (2¼in) at the hip.

Instructions

With colour A make 130ch on the Tunisian hook.

Row 1 Ts.
Row 2 Return row.
Row 3 6Ts. 15Tht. Ttr to end of row.
Row 4 Return row.
Row 5 Change to colour B. Tp.
Row 6 Return row.
Row 7 Change to colour A. Continue in stitch pattern until 16 panels have been worked.

To Complete the Last Panel

Row 1 As Row 1 of pattern.
Row 2 Return row.
Row 3 Ts.
Row 4 Return row.

To Make Up

Place right sides together. Using the ordinary crochet hook work 1 row of dc (sc), working into both edges, finishing at the hem. Work 1 row of dc (sc) around the hem. Work 1 row of crab st working from left to right. Finish off.

The Waistband

Use 3 ply botany wool and the ordinary crochet hook.
Row 1 Work dc (sc).
Row 2 Crab st into the front loop of the dc (sc).
Row 3 Work 1 row of dc (sc) into the back loop of the dc (sc) of row 1.
Row 4 dc (sc).
Row 5 As Row 4. Finish with 4ch.
Row 6 tr tr (dtr) into every stitch.
Sew the band into place at the back of the waist line.

Finishing Off

Press a fold on to every purl row of every panel. Thread the elastic through the waistband and sew the ends together.

Design 9: Striking Three-quarter-length Coat made with a Double-ended Hook
Illustrated in colour on page 57

Materials
700gm chunky (bulky) wool in the basic colour; 600gm yarns of assorted colours; for example, from Georges Picaud, Scheepjeswol, Rowan Yarns and Patons; No 7.00mm (K) double-ended Tunisian hook; No 6.00mm (I) crochet hook; 20cm of lining material for the pockets; 6 buttons; shoulder pads if desired.

Tension (Gauge)
13st to 10cm (4in).

Measurements
Length: 96cm (38in)
Bust: 107cm (42in)
Sleeve without cuff: 38cm (15in)
Cuff: 9cm (3½in)

Stitch Pattern
This is entirely optional. Use any stitches you like and turn the work every two rows. One side will be more colourful than the other, so you can choose the side you prefer as the right side.

Design Note
The garment you make will be entirely your own design, you can choose yarns which either tone or contrast with your basic colour. The coat is worked from the centre back and centre front to the side seams.

The design can be worked in three ways:
1 Use a regular stitch pattern and repeat it until the garment is completed.
2 Use a random stitch pattern, but making each side of the garment match as on the coat illustrated. To do this it is a good idea to use three Tunisian hooks and to work a few rows at a time on back and front alternately, because it is difficult to see or remember how you obtained the pattern.
3 Make the garment in a perfectly random fashion without the sides or sleeves matching.

Adaptations
To make a full-length coat add more stitches to the base chain at centre front and centre back. To make a shorter coat or jacket deduct stitches from the base chain. A wide sleeve with a turn-back cuff can be made by omitting the decreasing at the bottom of the sleeve and working a straight band of dc (sc) in the basic colour at the bottom of the sleeve.

Instructions
Left Back
Make 125ch in basic colour. Work in your own choice of yarn and stitch until back measures 19cm (7½in). sl st along 30st to make the armhole. Continue working for 7cm (2½in).
Shape the side seam by working from the armhole edge towards the hem in the following manner. sl st for 10st. Ts for 20st. Tht for 20st. Ttr to the end of the row. Work the return row. sl st to the end of the row to cast off (bind off).

Right Back
Return to the centre back and pick up the stitches on the base chain. Work the right back to match the left back.
Shape side seam by working 45Ttr, 20Tht and 20Ts. Work return row. sl st along row to cast off.

Left Front
Make 115ch in basic colour. Work in your chosen stitch and colour pattern for 8cm (3in). At the end of the return row add 10ch.
On the next row pick up and work stitch across the 10ch and continue in stitch to end of row. Continue until work measures 19cm (7½in).
Shape armhole by sl st 30st as on left back. Continue for 7cm (2½in) and shape side seam as on the back.

Right Front
Work to match left front.

Sleeves (make 2 worked sideways)
Make 52ch in basic colour. Work in your chosen stitch and colour pattern until sleeve measures 50cm (20in). Change to ordinary crochet hook. Work 1 row of dc (sc) along the row edges of one side for the top of the sleeve; this gives a firm edge when the sleeve is crocheted to the armhole.

Pockets (make 2)
Work in the basic colour with a stripe of another colour at the top.
Make 27ch in basic colour.
Row 1 Ttr.
Row 2 Turn work and attach another length of yarn of the basic colour. Return row.
Row 3 Ts.
Row 4 Turn work. Return row.

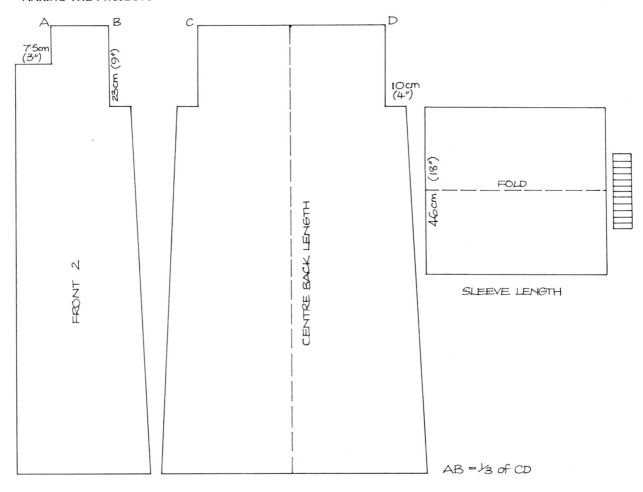

Fig 48

Continue for 10cm (4in) working 1 row of Ts and 1 row of Ttr.

Coloured Stripe
Row 1 Ttr.
Row 2 Return row in contrasting colour.
Row 3 3Ts, 1 Tdp tr to end of row.
Row 4 Return row.
Change to ordinary hook.
Row 5 dc (sc).
Row 6 Crab st. Finish off and run in ends.
Cut 2 pieces of lining material 1cm (½in) larger all round than the pocket. Turn in edges and oversew to the pocket, this reinforces it and helps to keep its shape. Sew lined pockets in position.

Edgings
Left Front
With right side of work facing and the ordinary crochet hook, work 3 rows dc (sc) from neck to hem.

Design 13: Simple-to-make sleeveless slipover worked in mohair (page 83)

Row 4 Work crab st on the front loop of st working from left to right.
Row 5 dc (sc) into the back loop of the st.

Right Front

Start at the bottom edge and work to the neck.
Row 1 dc (sc).
Row 2 Work button holes. 1ch, 1dc (sc). *3ch, miss 3st, 8dc (sc). Repeat from * 5 times, 3ch, miss 3st dc (sc) to the end of the row.
Row 3 dc (sc).
Row 4 Working from left to right, crab st on the front lp of the dc (sc).
Row 5 dc (sc) into the back lp of the st.

Collar

Sew up shoulder seams. With right side of work facing, start 1in in from the front at the neck. Pick up and work 58dc (sc) round the neck edge, taking 1tr each side into the square of the front neck. Work 6 more rows of dc (sc).
Edge collar with crab st into the front lp of the st and work a return row of dc (sc) into the back lp of the st.

To Make Up

Sew up shoulder seams. Find centre of sleeve and, with wrong sides together, pin to the shoulder seam. Pin each end of sleeve to the corner of the armhole. With right side of sleeve facing, work 1 row of dc (sc) through the sleeve and the coat. Turn to the wrong side and sew the top edge of each side of the sleeve to the armhole. Sew up sleeve seams.
Sew up side seams leaving 25cm (10in) open at the bottom if desired. Work 1 row of dc (sc) and 1 row of crab st around the bottom and side slits.

Cuffs

Work 1 row of dc (sc) around the bottom of the sleeve. Next row, take 2st together all round the cuff to decrease. Work 10 more rows.
Finish off with crab st edging as on the front edges.

Finishing Off

Sew on buttons. Reinforce button holes by working around them. Pull into shape and press with a cool iron if necessary. Add shoulder pads if desired.

Designs 14 and 15: Short-sleeved and long-sleeved jumpers made in random-dyed mohair (pages 85 and 86)

Design 10: Jumper in Hand-spun Wool with Deep Inset Sleeves
Illustrated in colour on page 58

Materials
Hand-spun wool dyed with natural vegetable dyes (for example from Ray Napier, 54 Neal Street, Covent Garden, London, WC2) – 200gm of colour A (grey), 200gm of colour B (natural) and 300gm of colour C (pink); No 6.00mm (I) Tunisian hook; No 6.00mm (I) crochet hook.
Note Any yarn of Aran thickness can be substituted.

Measurements
Length: 61cm (24in)
Bust: 108cm (42in)
Sleeve: 52cm (20½in)

Tension (Gauge)
15st to 10cm (4in).

Stitch Pattern
There are eight rows and three colours in this pattern. This means that the raised dtr blocks of three are in a different colour every time. If you use four colours instead of three the result will be quite different, with the colour pattern repeating itself every eight rows instead of every twenty-four rows.

To enlarge the jumper add more stitches in groups of six. To make the jumper smaller subtract stitches in groups of six. The blocks of dtr must balance each side of the jumper.

Row 1 Colour A, Ttr.
Row 2 Colour B, return row.
Row 3 Colour B, Tp.
Row 4 Colour C, return row.
Row 5 Colour C, Ttr.
Row 6 Colour A, return row.
Row 7 * 3Tp, 3dtr picking up the lp of the p stitch of Row 3. Repeat from *.
Row 8 Colour B, return row.
Rows 1 to 8 form pattern
Continue working these 8 rows with the colours in the same order, changing the colour on the left.

Design Note
The welt and wrist edgings are worked sideways, crocheted into a circle and joined on after the jumper has been sewn up.

Instructions
The back and front are made in the same way.
Using colour A make 77ch on the Tunisian hook.
Row 1 Into the 4th ch from the hook work 1Ttr. Ttr to end of row.
Row 2 Return row.
Continue working in the stitch and colour pattern for 27cm (10½in), 38 rows.
If you wish to lengthen the garment work more rows at this point.

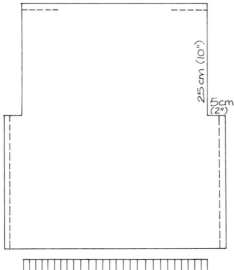

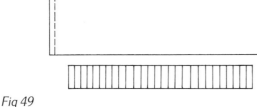

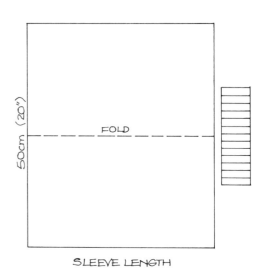

Fig 49

SLEEVE LENGTH

Armhole Shaping

sl st across 8st. Work in stitch pattern leaving 8st at the end of the row. Continue working in stitch and colour pattern for 23cm (9in). Using colour A and the ordinary crochet hook work 6 rows of dc (sc) taking every stitch into the back lp of the stitch of the previous row. Finish off.

Sleeves (make 2)

These are worked from the armhole down to the wrist. Using colour A make 93ch on the Tunisian hook. Work in stitch and colour pattern for 14 rows. Decrease every other row by working the 2nd and 3rd st together at the beginning of the row and the 2nd and 3rd st together before the end of the row. Continue in pattern until 56st remain. Decrease at each end of every 4th row until 48st remain.

To Shape for Cuff

Using colour B and the ordinary crochet hook, work 1 row of decreasing by working 1dc (sc) and 2dc (sc) tog to the end of the row.

Waistband

Using colour C make 19ch.
Row 1 dc (sc) into every ch. 1ch.
Row 2 dc (sc) into the back of every st.
Repeat these rows until the waistband measures 77cm

(30in). Place the base ch along the last row and crochet together to make a circle.

Cuffs (make 2)

Make 14ch. Work as for waistband until strip is 20cm (8in). Crochet into a circle.

To Make Up

Place wrong sides together and crochet across the top to make the shoulder seams and the boat-shaped neck. Work 14dc (sc) for the left shoulder seam. Continue dc (sc) across the front of the neck and 14dc (sc) for the right shoulder seam. Finish off. Rejoin wool to the back of the neck and work 1 row of dc (sc) to match the front neck. Work all around the neck in crab st.

Sleeve Seams

Work one row of dc (sc) to tidy the armhole edge. Pin the centre of the sleeve top to the shoulder seam. With sleeve nearest, crochet sleeve to the armhole with one row of dc (sc).
Sew the bottom of the armhole to the side of the sleeve on both sides. Oversew sleeve and side seams.

Waistband and Cuffs

Place waistband over the bottom of the jumper and join with 1 row of dc (sc). Attach cuffs to the sleeves in the same way.

Design 11: Cushion in Tunisian Crochet made with a Double-ended Hook

Illustrated in colour on page 36

Materials
150gm of natural sheep wool in 2 colours; No 7.00mm (K) double-ended Tunisian hook; No 6 (I) crochet hook; 1 36cm (14in) cushion pad
Note The wool used for the cushion illustrated came from the Black Sheep Shop (see Appendix 4). Any Aran (fisherman) wool can be substituted.

Measurements
36cm (14in) square.

Tension (Gauge)
15st to 10cm (4in).

Stitch Pattern
Row 1 Ts, turn the work and push to the other end of the hook.
Row 2 Colour B, return row.
Row 3 Ts.
Row 4 Colour A, return row.

Rows 1 to 4 form pattern
The stitch is quite simple. Before every return row, push the work to the end of the hook, turn, and pick up the new colour. A fabric is produced which looks the same stitch on each side, but one side is light and the other dark.

Instructions
Using colour A make 48ch. Work in stitch pattern until a square is completed. Cast off (bind off) with a sl st. Work 1 row of dc (sc) all around the square in the colour of your choice. Make a second square.

To Make Up
Place the two squares together and dc (sc) the edges together on three sides. Insert the cushion pad and dc (sc) along the fourth side.

Design 12: Cushion Cover Embroidered in Cross Stitch with a Traditional Rose Design

Illustrated in colour on page 48

Materials
150gm of Aran (fisherman) wool or any wool of Aran (fisherman) thickness; No 7.00mm (K) Tunisian hook; 1 36cm (14in) sq cushion pad; 1 skein each of a pale blue, dark blue, old rose, medium pink, pale pink, light green, dark green and yellow embroidery wool

Measurements
36cm (14in) square.

Tension
17st and 15 rows to 10cm (4in).

Stitch
The cushion is worked in Tunisian simple (Afghan stitch) throughout. This is used as an embroidery canvas, the squares forming a base for cross-stitch embroidery.

Adaptations
Two identical squares are worked for the front and back of the cushion, but if preferred the back of the cushion can be made of a contrasting material. Two embroidered squares can be made into a tote bag by adding a handle. Twenty squares, all embroidered and joined together with double (single) crochet will make a bed cover or rug (Afghan).

Instructions
The back and front are made in the same way.
Make 56ch Ts into every stitch until 48 rows, with return rows, have been completed.

Finishing Off
Embroider with cross stitch as shown in the chart.

Cord for Edging
Take 8 strands of various colours 115cm (65in) long and, with a friend, twist both ends as tightly as possible. Fold in half and it will twist into a cord. Sew the cord to the edge of the cushion.

A chart for the cross stitch embroidery is given on page 82.

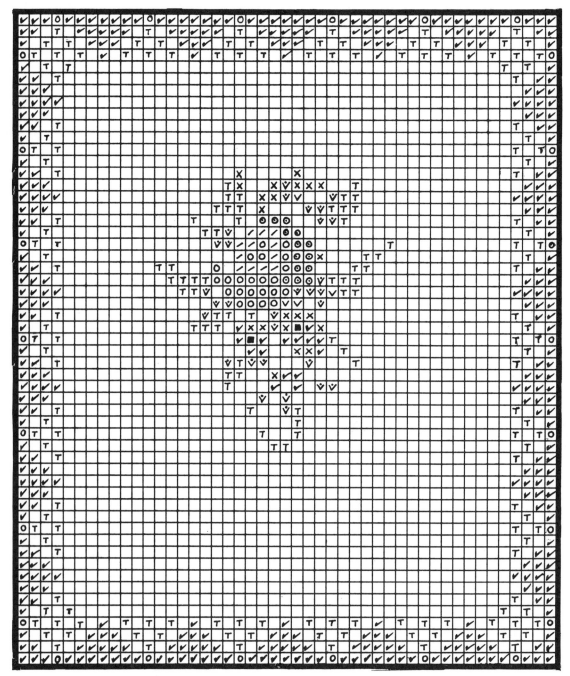

⊠ Pale blue   ☑ Pink
☑ Dark blue   ⊤ Light green
⊙ Old rose   ☑ Dark green
◎ Medium pink   ■ Yellow

Fig 50

Design 13: Simple-to-make, Sleeveless Slipover in Mauve and Heather Shades
Illustrated in colour on page 75

Materials
3×50gm balls Georges Picaud Filatura di Crosa; 25.00mm wooden or plastic broomstick; No 4.50mm (G) crochet hook; No 3¼mm (3) knitting needles for knitted rib.

Note Other mohair can be substituted, but first test the yarn to make sure it is easy to work with.

Measurements
Length: 56cm (22in)
Bust: 92–102cm (36–40in)
To increase the size add more stitches in multiples of 2.

Tension (Gauge)
5½ rows to 10cm (4in)
5grps of broomstick lps to 10cm (4in). Measurements are given for rows.

Stitch
Working from left to right, place hook into the back of the stitch, pull loop through and place on broomstick. Remove loops in groups of 2 or 3 with 2 or 3 dc (sc).

Design Note
The garment is made from a rectangle and the rib at the waist gives the shaping. The ribs are made first and can be worked in knitting (kl, pl) or in crochet dc (sc) worked into the back of the loop in every stitch and every row, making a long strip which can be turned on its side to make a waistband. See Fig 51 overleaf.

Instructions
The back and front are made in the same way.

Knitted Rib
Cast on 72st. Work kl, pl for 9cm (3½in). Change to crochet hook.
Row 1 Place the broomstick parallel with the knitting needle. Put the hook into each stitch and pull up a loop, placing it on to the broomstick (72lps).

Crochet Rib
Make 16ch.
Row 1 dc (sc).
Row 2 dc (sc) into the back lp of every st to the end of the row.
Repeat Row 2 until 72 rows have been worked. Turn the long strip on to its side and place the last lp on to the broomstick. Pick up 72lps and place on to the broomstick.

Body
Remove the lps in groups of 2 with 2 dc (sc).
Work in broomstick stitch until 14 complete rows have been worked.
Finish off.

To Make Up
Sewing Up
Place right sides together and sew up the side seams, taking 2 oversewing st on the dc (sc) row and leaving lp in between. Leave 20cm (8in) for the armholes. Sew along 8lps each side for the shoulder.

Crocheting Together
By crocheting together it is possible to wear the garment with either side as the right side. Use dc (sc) into the dc (sc) rows with 4ch in between (see page 41).

Finishing Off
Neck edging
Work 1 row of dc (sc) around the neck edge.

Armhole Edging
Row 1 Work 2dc (sc) into the dc row then 4ch across the lp row.
Row 2 Work 1 row of dc (sc) into every ch and dc (sc).

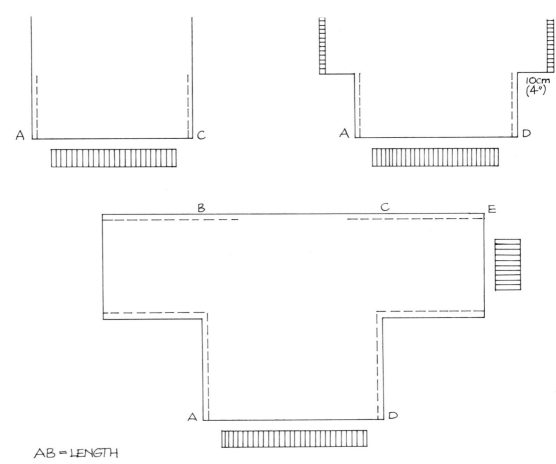

AB = LENGTH

CE = SLEEVE LENGTH

AD = ½ BUST MEASUREMENT

Fig 51

Design 14: Short-sleeved T-shaped Jumper in Random-dyed Seascape Colours

Illustrated in colour on page 76 (see also Fig 51)

Materials
4×50gm balls Georges Picaud Filatura di Crosa; 25.00mm wooden or plastic broomstick; No 4.50mm (C) crochet hook; No 3¼mm (3) knitting needles for knitted rib.

Note Other mohair can be substituted, but first test the yarn to make sure it is easy to work with.

Measurements
Length: 56cm (22in)
Bust: 81–92cm (32–36in)

Tension (Gauge)
15st to 10cm (4in), 5½ rows of broomstick lps to 10cm (4in).

Instructions
The back and front are made in the same way.
Work as for Design 13, but grouping 3lps together with 3dc (sc) to make a smaller size, until 7 complete rows of broomstick lps have been worked.

Magyar Sleeves (make 2)
Row 1 Add 21ch to the end of the last row worked for the left sleeve. Attach 21ch to the right side of the work for the right sleeve. Work across the extra stitches, picking up extra loops each side. Work in broomstick stitch until 14 complete rows have been worked from the beginning.

To Make Up
Sew or crochet together as described for Design 13.

Sleeve Edging
Row 1 Work dc (sc) into the dc (sc) rows with 4ch in between.
Row 2 Work dc (sc) into every stitch.
For a knitted edging, pick up and knit 1st into every crochet stitch. Knit 6 rows of k1, p1 rib.

Design 15: Long-sleeved Mohair Jumper with Knitted Welts in Russet Shades
Illustrated in colour on page 76 (see also Fig 51)

Materials
4×50gm balls Georges Picaud Filatura di Crosa; 25.00mm wooden or plastic broomstick; No 4.50mm (G) crochet hook; No 3¼mm (3) knitting needles for knitted rib.

Note Other mohair can be substituted, but first test the yarn to make sure it is easy to work with.

Measurements
Length: 56cm (22in)
Bust: 81–92cm (32–36in)

Tension (Gauge)
5grps of broomstick lps to 10cm (4in), 5½ rows of broomstick lps to 10cm (4in).

Instructions
The back and front are made in the same way as Designs 13 and 14.

With knitted ribs, work as for Design 13 until 8 complete broomstick rows have been made.

Sleeves (make 2)
Add 54ch to the last row of broomstick lps for the left sleeve. Attach 54ch to the other side of the work for the right sleeve. Continue in broomstick st working across the extra stitches until 14 complete rows have been worked from the beginning.

To Make Up
Sew up or crochet together as described for Design 13.

Sleeve Edging
Work round the bottom of the sleeves with dc (sc) into the dc (sc) rows and 4ch in between. Work a second row crocheting or knitting 2st together. Work a 7.5cm (3in) cuff in either dc (sc) or k1, p1 rib. If the cuff is crocheted, attach cuff to the bottom of the sleeve with 1 row of dc (sc).

Design 16: Heavily-fringed Stole

Materials
200gm of mohair; 25.00mm broomstick; No 4.50mm (G) crochet hook.
Note If you decide to use a thicker yarn to make a stole to wear over a coat, more yarn will be necessary. It is possible to estimate how much after using up the first ball.

Tension (Gauge)
Accurate tension is not important in scarves and shawls.

Instructions
Make 120ch. Work 42 complete broomstick rows,

removing loops in groups of 3 with 3dc (sc).

Finishing Off
Cut wool into strips twice as long as you would like the fringe, plus 2.5cm (1in). Take 4 pieces together, fold in half and, using a hook, pull the looped end through the crochet. Hook the ends through the loop and pull tight.

Adaptations
The size of the stole is entirely up to the maker as it is only a long, straight strip of broomstick crochet with the ends fringed. A shorter, narrower version will make a scarf.

Design 17: Slim-fitting Button-through Scarlet Waistcoat
Illustrated in colour on page 94

Materials
400gm of a double double or chunky (bulky) yarn; 25.00mm broomstick; No 5.00mm (H) crochet hook; 8 buttons.

Tension (Gauge)
4grps of broomstick lps to 10cm (4in), 5½ broomstick rows to 10cm (4in).

Measurements
Length: 48cm (19in)
Bust: 97cm (38in)

Stitch
Broomstick Crochet, 3lps worked together with 3dc (sc).

Adaptations
This is a waist-hugging style but it can be lengthened to a hip-line waistcoat to wear with trousers. The back and fronts are worked in one piece as far as the armholes. The garment can be made longer by adding more rows before it is divided for the armholes.

Back and Fronts
Make 144ch.
Row 1 Place the last lp on to the broomstick and pick up 1lp in every ch.
Row 2 Take off the lps in groups of 3 with 3 dc (sc). Work straight until 9 rows of lps have been completed.

To Divide for the Armholes
Left Yoke
Row 1 Pick up 30lps.
Row 2 Take off lps in groups of 3 and work until 5 rows of lps have been completed.
Row 11 Turn work round to the wrong side and sl st along 10st. Place the last lp on to the broomstick and pick up lps to the end of the row.

Work until 3 rows of lps have been completed and finish off.

Back Yoke
Return to the armhole row. Miss 4grps and attach yarn. Pick up 60lps.
Row 2 Remove lps in grps of 3.
Work straight until 8 rows of lps have been completed.

Right Yoke
Return to armhole row. Miss 4grps and attach yarn. Work to match left yoke.

To Make Up
Wrong sides together, place front shoulders in position on the back and crochet together with dc (sc).

Armhole Edging
Row 1 Start in the centre of the armhole at the bottom and work 1 dc (sc) into every st. Around the edge of the broomstick rows, work 4ch across the lps and 1 dc (sc) into the dc (sc) row.
Row 2 1 row of dc (sc) around the armhole working into every st and ch.

Complete Edging
Row 1 Start at the centre back of neck and dc (sc) into every st to the shoulder. Work the edge all around the garment in the same manner as the armholes, working dc (sc) into the dc (sc) rows and 4ch over the lps. sl st to the first dc (sc) at the back of the neck.
Row 2 Mark the position of the buttonholes with coloured cotton.
Work all round the garment with dc (sc) into every st but missing 2st and working 2ch for every buttonhole.

Finishing Off
Work buttonhole stitch around every buttonhole loop. Sew buttons on. Do not press.

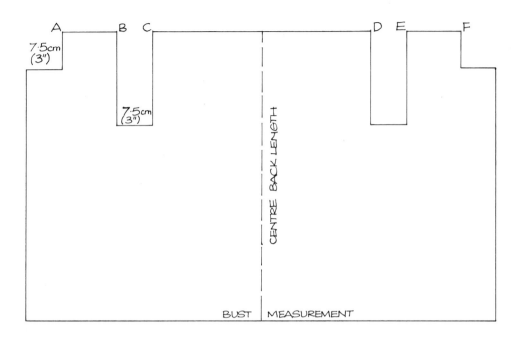

AB and EF = ⅓ of CD

Fig 52

Design 18, 19, 20 and 21: Broomstick Crochet for a Wedding
Illustrated in colour on page 93

Materials

Thick crochet or knitting cotton such as Twilleys Stalite – the bride's head-dress, the Juliet cap and the handbag all take less than 1 ball, the picture hat takes 2 balls; 20.00mm broomstick; No 3.50mm (E) crochet hook; 1m (40in) of millinery or florists wire and 65cm (25in) of petersham for the hat; 1m (40in) millinery or florists' wire for the bride's headdress, beads, flowers and ribbon for decoration; a 15cm (6in) silver bag frame (obtainable from needlework shops) and 15cm (6in) lining material for the bag.

Choose colours to complement the theme.

Tension (Gauge)

5grps of broomstick lps to 10cm (4in).

Stiffening

Dissolve 1 cup of sugar in ½ cup of water and bring to the boil. Soak hat in the solution and squeeze out. Pull into shape, place over suitable mould such as a wig stand or pudding basin and place on a board to dry. This takes about two weeks and cannot be hurried. If the hats do get damp and lose their shape, remove the trimmings and thoroughly dampen down, remould into shape, dry and retrim.

Design 18: Bride's Head-dress

Instructions

Make 58ch.

Row 1 1tr (dc) into 3rd ch from hook. 1tr (dc) into every ch (56 bars).

Row 2 Place the lp on to the broomstick and pick up 1lp into every tr (dc) and 4lps into the turning ch at the end of the row.

Row 3 1ch the first grp of 4lps; 4dc (sc) into the same grp. Continue to the end of the row, removing lps in grps of 4 with 4dc (sc). Finish off by cutting the cotton and pull through the last lp.

Row 4 Turn work upside down; join on and pick up lps into the base of the tr (dc). Pick up 4lps into the side of the last stitch.

Row 5 As Row 3.

Row 6 Work 1 row of dc (sc) into the top of the Broomstick Crochet all the way round, enclosing a length of millinery wire at the same time. Finish off and run in ends. Decorate in any way you wish with beads or pearls. This must be done before it is stiffened as it becomes very hard and difficult to sew once the sugar solution has dried. Stiffen and dry as described on page 90, using a round box as a mould and pinning into shape.

Adaptations

This head-dress can be worn as a coronet or halo. Flowers may be preferred as a decoration.

Design 19: Bridesmaid's Juliet Cap

Instructions

Make 6ch.

Row 1 Place the last lp on to the broomstick and into the 6ch pick up 17 more lps.

Row 2 Take lps off the broomstick in grps of 3 with 6dc (sc) into each group (6grps).

Row 3 Pull up 1lp into every dc (sc) (36lps).

Row 4 As Row 2 (12grps).

Row 5 As Row 3.

Row 6 As Row 2 (24grps).

Rows 7 to 12 Work straight in broomstick stitch, working 3lps together with 3dc (sc).

To Finish Off

Sew into a circle taking oversewing stitches into the dc (sc) rows and leaving loops over the loop rows. Stiffen and dry as described on page 90.

Adaptations

This also makes an attractive adult's hat worn at an angle and decorated with veiling and a spray of flowers or fruit.

Design 20: Wide-brimmed Hat for Weddings and Special Occasions

Instructions
Make 6ch.
Row 1 Place the last lp on to the broomstick and into the 6ch pick up 17 more lps.
Row 2 Take lps off the broomstick in grps of 3 with 6dc (sc) into each grp (6grps).
Row 3 Pull up 1lp into every dc (sc) (36lps).
Row 4 As Row 2 (12grps).
Row 5 As Row 3.
Row 6 As Row 2 (24grps).
Row 7 As Row 3.
Row 8 No increasing. Work 3dc (sc) into every grp of 3lps.
Row 9 As Row 3.
Row 10 Take off each grp of 3 with 4dc (sc).
Row 11 As Row 3.
Row 12 Take off each grp of 4 with 4dc (sc).
Row 13 As Row 3.

The Brim
Row 14 Work 6dc (sc) into every grp.
Row 15 As Row 3.
Row 16 Work 3dc (sc) into each grp of 3, doubling the number of grps for the brim.
Row 17 As Row 3.
Row 18 Work 4dc (sc) into every grp of 3lps.
Row 19 As Row 3.
Row 20 Work 5dc (sc) into every group of 4.
Row 21 Make the millinery wire into a circle for the edge of the brim by twisting the ends round each other. Into the dc (sc) of the last broomstick lps, and over the millinery wire, work 1 row of dc (sc).

Finishing Off
Sew up as explained for the Juliet Cap (design 19). Stiffen and dry as described on page 90. Sew in the petersham, adjusting this to the size required. Decorate with ribbon and flowers.

Design 18: Bride's head-dress decorated with pearl beads (page 91)
Design 19: Bridesmaid's juliet cap (page 91)
Design 20: Wide-brimmed hat for weddings and special occasions (above)
Design 21: Small broomstick crochet bag (page 95)

Design 21: Small Bag

Instructions
The bag is made of 2 rectangles of Broomstick Crochet. Make 38ch.

Row 1 Place last lp on broomstick and pull up lps in the usual way.

Row 2 Take off lps in grps of 3 with 3dc (sc). Continue in broomstick stitch until 6 complete rows have been worked.

To Make Up
Crochet the 2 bottom rows together with dc (sc). Cut 2 bags in lining material 2.5cm (1in) bigger than the crochet. Machine the linings and put them together with seams inside. Oversew the edges together and sew to the back of the bag frame. Place the crochet bag over the lining and sew in place with a matching thread.

Adaptations
For an evening bag use thick lurex thread such as Twilleys double gold fingering.

Design 17: Slim-fitting button-through waistcoat (page 88)

Design 23: Peter Pan collar (page 99)

Design 22: Dramatic Evening Coat with Very Full Sleeves
Illustrated in colour on page 111

Materials
13×50gm balls Georges Picaud No 1 Kid Mohair; No 6.00mm (I) Tunisian hook; 25.00mm broomstick; No 6.00mm (I) crochet; reel of fine silver embroidery thread available at needlework shops; fancy buckle or attractive buttons.

Measurements
Length: 102cm (48in)
Width across yoke: 43cm (17in)
Sleeves: 49cm (19in)

Tension (Gauge)
Tunisian: 16st and 30 rows to 10cm (4in)
Broomstick: 6grps and 2⅞ broomstick rows to 10cm (4in)

Stitch Pattern
Row 1 1Tp, 1Ts.
Row 2 Return row.
Row 3 1Ts, 1Tp.
Row 4 Return row.
Rows 1 to 4 form pattern
This stitch is similar to moss stitch in knitting.
Broomstick loops are worked in the usual way with 3dc (sc) removing 3lps unless otherwise stated.
Crab stitch makes the edging of the collar.

Design Note
The yokes are worked first in Tunisian stitch, then the broomstick loops are picked up at the bottom of the yokes and broomstick stitch is worked from the top to the bottom. The silver embroidery thread is used with the mohair for the yokes, cuffs and edgings.

Adaptations
A shortened version with no lurex thread would make an attractive bed jacket. A full length version can be made by adding more rows of Broomstick Crochet.

Instructions
Back Yoke
Using the mohair with the silver thread, make 68ch.
Row 1 Ts.
Row 2 Return row.
Row 3 Tp.
Row 4 As Row 2.
Row 5 As Row 3.
Row 6 As Row 2.
Row 7 Start stitch pattern of 1Tp, 1Ts.
Row 8 Return row.
Row 9 1Ts, 1Tp.

Row 10 Return row.
Rows 7 to 10 form pattern
Work in stitch until 13cm (5in) have been completed. Finish off.

Right Yoke
Make 34ch. Work to match the back yoke until 14 rows have been completed.
Row 15 sl st over 9st and complete the row in stitch pattern.
Row 16 Return row.
Row 17 sl st over 3st and complete the row in pattern. Continue in pattern until the front yoke is the same length as the back yoke.

Left Yoke
Make 34ch. Work 14 rows as for the right yoke.
Row 15 Work in stitch pattern over 25st. sl st to end of row. Break yarn and rejoin to the end of the stitches on the hook.
Row 16 Return row.
Row 17 Work in stitch pattern and sl st the last 3st. Break yarn and rejoin to the stitches on the needle.
Row 18 Return row.
Work in pattern until the left yoke matches the right yoke.

Back
Use the mohair.
Row 1 Pick up broomstick loops with broomstick and an ordinary crochet hook into every stitch at the bottom of the yoke.
Row 2 Remove loops 2 at a time with 2dc (sc).
Row 3 As Row 1.
Row 4 As Row 2.
Row 5 As Row 1.
Row 6 Remove loops with 3dc (sc) into every 2 loops. Leave work on one side.

Right and Left Fronts
Using the mohair, pick up and work broomstick loops as described for the back and until 6 rows have been completed.

Joining Together at the Armholes
The sections are joined together at the bottom of the armholes so that the main part of the coat is worked in one piece.
Make 12ch at the end of the last row of the left front and 12ch at the end of the last row of the back.
Row 1 Join the yokes to the back by picking up the loops across the left front, along the 12ch attached to

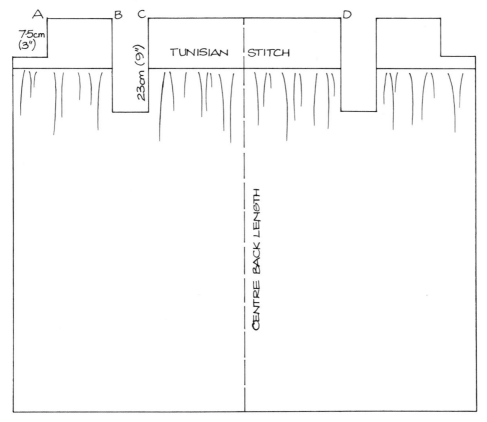

A   B C   D

7.5cm
(3")

23cm (9")   TUNISIAN   STITCH

CENTRE BACK LENGTH

Fig 53

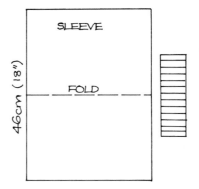

SLEEVE

46cm (18")   FOLD

AB = 1/3 of CD

the back, across the back and along the 12ch attached to the right front.

Row 2 Return row, removing 3 lps with 3dc (sc). Continue working broomstick loops until another 24 complete rows of loops have been worked. Adjust the length at this point by working more rows if necessary.

Sleeves (make 2)

84ch. Work in broomstick st of 3lps taken off with 3dc (sc) until 12 rows of loops have been completed.

Cuffs

Use mohair and silver thread.

Row 1 Change to a Tunisian hook. Pick up every other lp, making 42 lps on hook.

Row 2 Return row.

Row 3 With Tp work 2 tog 4 times at each end of the row (34lps).

Row 4 Return row.

Row 5 Tp.

Row 6 Return row.

Row 7 Work in the stitch pattern of 1Tp, 1Ts.

Continue in stitch pattern for 20 rows and finish off with 1 row of sl st.

Collar

Sew up the shoulder seams.

Row 1 Right side of work facing, using Tunisian hook and mohair with silver thread, miss first 3st and pick up stitches around the neck edge leaving the last 3st of the left front.

Row 2 Return row.

Row 3 Ts.

Row 4 Return row.

Row 5 Work in the stitch pattern of 1Tp, 1Ts.

Continue in stitch pattern, until 12 rows have been completed.

Edging

With an ordinary crochet hook, join yarn and silver thread to the bottom front edge of the left yoke. Work crab st from left to right along the yoke, round the collar and down the edge of the right yoke.

Continue with the same yarn and work down the front edge of the coat with 3ch across every space and 1dc (sc) into the dc (sc) row. Continue with dc (sc) along the hem line and 3ch, 1dc (sc) along the left front edge until the yoke where the crab stitch begins. Turn work. Work 1 row of dc (sc) along the edge back to the right yoke and finish off.

To Make Up

Sew or crochet shoulder seams together. Mark centre of sleeve and place on the shoulder seam. Sew head of sleeve into position. Turn work inside out and sew 4cm (1½in) of each side seam to the underarm of the coat. Sew up the sleeve seams. Work crab st around the edge of the cuff.

Finishing Off

Run in all ends. Press with a cool iron. Sew buckle on to the yoke. Shoulder pads can be added if necessary.

Design 23: Peter Pan Collar
Illustrated in colour on page 94

Materials
1 ball Twilleys Stalite or similar thick cotton (1 ball makes 2 collars); 20.00mm broomstick; No 3.50mm (E) crochet hook.

Instructions
Make 72ch.

Row 1 Pick up 1lp in every ch over the broomstick.

Row 2 Remove the first 3lps with 1ch. 4dc (sc) into 3lps to the end of the row (24grps).

Row 3 Pick up the lps (96lps).

Row 4 Remove the first 4lps with 1ch. 5dc (sc) into 4lps to the end of the row.

Row 5 Pick up the lps.

Row 6 Remove 5lps with 6dc (sc). Finish off.

Neck Ties and Edging
With right side of collar facing, attach cotton to the base ch and work 48ch. sl st along the 48ch. Into the base ch of collar work 1 row of dc (sc). Add 48ch to the other end of collar and sl st back to the beginning.

The neck ties can be omitted if the collar is to be sewn or pinned to the dress.

Design 24: Circular Cushion in Broomstick Crochet
Illustrated in colour on page 36

Materials
100gm natural wool (colour A); 50gm black wool (colour B); 25.00mm broomstick; No 6.00mm (I) crochet hook.

Note The wool used for the cushion illustrated came from the Black Sheep Shop (see Appendix 4). Any yarn of Aran (fisherman) thickness can be substituted.

Measurements
Diameter: 36cm (14in)
Depth: 10cm (4in)

Stitch Pattern
Broomstick groups of stitches, increasing every row so as to form a circle.

Instructions
Using colour A make 6ch.
Row 1 Place the lp on to the broomstick and pull up 17 more lps through the ch to the broomstick.
Row 2 Remove lps in grps of 3 with 6dc (sc).
Row 3 Colour B, place last lp on to broomstick and pick up 1lp into every dc (sc).
Row 4 As Row 2.
Row 5 Colour A, as Row 3.
Row 6 As Row 2.
Row 7 Colour B, pick up lps. Do not increase on this row.
Row 8 Remove lps in grps of 3 with 3dc (sc).
Row 9 Colour A, pick up lps.
Row 10 Remove lps in grps of 3 with 4dc (sc).
Row 11 Change to ordinary crochet hook and work 1 row of dc (sc) into the back lp of every stitch.
Work another circle in the same way.

Side Panel
Using colour B make 175ch.
Row 1 Into 4th ch from hook work 1tr (dc). Work in tr (dc) to the end of the row.
Row 2 Colour A, place last lp on to the broomstick and pull up 1lp into every st on to the broomstick to the end of the row.
Row 3 Remove lps in grps of 3 with 4dc (sc).
Row 4 Change to ordinary crochet hook and work 1dc (sc) into the top of every broomstick lp. Finish off.
Return to the other side of the tr (dc) in colour B. Attach colour A and pick up broomstick lps into every tr (dc) stitch. Remove lps in grps of 3 with 4dc (sc). Change to ordinary crochet hook and work 1 row of dc (sc).

To Make Up
Sew up into circles and sew the side panel into a ring. With wrong sides together place the side panel around the edge of one circle and crochet into place with dc (sc).
Make a cushion pad the same size as the cushion measurements. Place into position and crochet the second circle on to the side panel. To wash the cushion cover, unpick the side panel far enough to remove the cushion pad. After washing replace pad and crochet into place.

Design 25: Thick Blanket made on a Rug-length Broomstick
Illustrated in colour on page 112

The blanket illustrated is being made of chunky (bulky) wool in five colours in autumnal shades of brown, rust, green, natural and beige.

A blanket is just a large rectangle of Broomstick Crochet worked on a 60cm (24in) long blanket broomstick and needs no pattern. If you are making it in a variety of different colours to use up odd wool it is best to have one basic colour, say black, brown or white, and use this for every other row. You can still use up oddments of the base colour, but having a little order in the colour arrangement gives a better effect. You can, of course, choose colours to match your furnishings.

Make a basic chain as wide as you wish the blanket to be and remove the lps in grps of 4 or 5. Work until the blanket is as big as required. Make a multi-coloured fringe on each end if desired.

Design 26: Triangular and Circular Shawls

A Circular Shawl

This can be worked with a 20mm broomstick and a No 3.00mm (C) crochet hook in fine baby wool. A thicker version can be made with a 25.00mm broomstick, a No 5 (H) crochet hook and thick wool. The instructions are the same but the thicker shawl will grow more quickly and take more yarn. The quantities required will depend on the yarn used and the size required.

Instructions
Make 6ch.
Row 1 Place the last lp on the broomstick and pick up 17 more lps.
Row 2 1ch into the first grp of 3lps. 6dc (sc) into every grp of 3 to the end of the row.
Row 3 Pick up 1lp into every dc (sc).
Row 4 As Row 2.
Row 5 As Row 3.
Continue working Rows 2 and 3 increasing the number of stitches every row until the shawl is as large as you wish.

Finishing Off
Make into a circle by sewing the ends of the rows together with oversewing stitches into the dc (sc) rows. Pull into shape. If pressing is necessary, use a warm iron over a dry cloth.
If you would like a fringe on the shawl, make as for design 16.

A Triangular Shawl

This shawl is made from the point at the bottom, working up to the top edge. It can be as large or as small as you like. Use a 20mm broomstick for fine wool and a 25.00mm broomstick for thick wool.

Instructions
Make 4ch. Place the lp on to the broomstick.
Row 1 Into the ch work 7 more lps.
Row 2 Remove the 1st 4lps with 1ch. 8dc (sc). Remove the 2nd 4lps with 8dc (sc).
Row 3 Pick up lp in every dc (sc) (16lps).
Row 4 8dc (sc) into the 1st 4lps. (4dc (sc) into the next 4lps) twice. 8dc (sc) into the last 4lps.
Continue working, increasing at the beginning and end of every dc (sc) row until the shawl is as large as you wish.

Edging
Row 1 Work an edging along the two sides of the triangle by working 1dc (sc) into the dc (sc) row with 4ch in between.
Row 2 Work 1 row of dc (sc) into every ch.
Add fringe if desired, following instructions for design 16.

Detail of fringing a triangular shawl

BASIC CROCHET STITCHES

Slip Stitch sl st

1 Make a length of chain.
2 Insert hook into 2nd st next to hook.
3 yrh (yo).
4 Pull lp through st and through lp on hook at the same time. (This st has no depth and so requires no tch.)

Slip stitch is used for joining chains into a circle or for travelling along the work when decreasing a number of stitches together, for example for an armhole.

Fig 54

Double Crochet dc (Single Crochet sc)

1 1tch.
2 Insert hook into 2nd st.
3 yrh (yo).
4 Pull thread through. 2lps on hook.
5 yrh (yo) and pull through the 2lps.
6 Repeat into next st.

Fig 55

Double (single) crochet is used for edgings. It makes a firm tight fabric but it is not often used for garments on its own. It is usually part of a stitch pattern. Try working the stitch but always inserting the hook into the back loop of the stitch. This makes a very satisfactory crochet rib but it is worked sideways and has to be sewn or crocheted on to the garment or, alternatively, work the ribbing, turn it sideways and crochet along the ends of the rows.

Fig 56

Half Treble htr (Half Double Crochet hdc)

Make 2tch.
1 yrh (yo).
2 Insert hook into 2nd st.
3 yrh (yo) and pull through 1lp. 3lps on hook.
4 yrh (yo) and pull through 3lps.
Continue working into every stitch.
This makes a firm, thick stitch suitable for jackets.

Fig 57

Fig 58

Double Treble dtr (Treble tr)

Make 4tch.
1   yrh (yo) twice.
2   Insert hook into 2nd st.
3   yrh (yo) and pull through. 4lps on hook.
4   yrh (yo) and pull through 2lps. 3lps on hook.
5   Repeat step 4. 2lps on hook.
6   Repeat step 4.
This is a taller stitch and is used for lacy patterns and textured crochet.

Treble Crochet tr (Double Crochet dc)

1   Notice that the chain is a loop with a strand passing from it to the next stitch. When working place the hook into the bottom of the chain making two threads on the hook.
2   yrh (yo).
3   Insert hook into 4th ch from hook.
4   yrh (yo) and pull through 1lp.
5   yrh (yo) and pull through 2lps.
6   yrh (yo) and pull through 2lps.
7   yrh (yo) and insert hook into next ch. Repeat steps 4, 5 and 6.

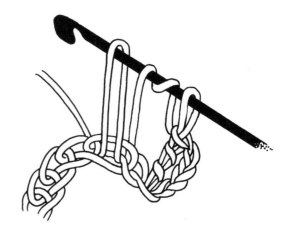

Fig 61

Fig 59

Triple Treble tr tr (Double Treble dtr)

Make 5tch.
1   yrh (yo) three times.
2   Insert hook into 2nd st.
3   yrh (yo) and pull through. 5lps on hook.
4   yrh (yo) and pull through 2lps. 4lps on hook.
5   Repeat step 4 three times until 1lp remains on hook.
It is possible to continue making trebles as long as you like by putting the yarn round the hook more times but this is just common sense and does not need further explanation. A triple treble would make a satisfactory belt loop.

Fig 60

Fig 62

Turning Chain (tch)

Turning chain is the chain at the end of the row to accommodate the height of the stitch. Some commercial patterns give this at the beginning of the row and others at the end. To obtain a firm straight edge to your work count the turning chain as the first stitch.

Consequently, when the work is turned, it makes the last stitch of the previous row and so a stitch must always be worked into it. This is not always easy but to make a firm edge a stitch should be worked into the turning chain rather than the space between the turning chain and the last stitch. Sometimes when working trebles there is a small hole at the end of every other row. This is because the turning chain is loose, perhaps through thick yarn or a slack tension. To correct this use two turning chain instead of three at the end of the row. Some patterns give two turning chain for trebles and some will give three. Experience will help you to find out whether your tension needs two or three stitches.

Turning chain	Number of chain
Slip stitch (sl st)	0
Double crochet (dc)	1
Half treble (htr)	2
Treble (tr)	2 or 3
Double treble (dtr)	4
Triple treble (ttr)	5
Quadruple treble (quad tr)	6 and so on

The work can be kept straight and even at the edges whatever the stitch by following the advice below. This applies to crochet in one stitch only. When working to complicated patterns the instructions will give guidance on how to keep a straight edge.

Keeping the Edges Straight

1 At the end of first row of tr (dc) make 3ch. These are called turning chain (tch). Turn work.
2 Hold tch at right angles to row completed and you will see that this 3ch will count as the first st.
3 1tr into the 2nd st and 1tr into every st to the end of the row making 1tr into the 3rd tch of the previous row, 3ch and turn.
4 Repeat the previous row.
The secret of keeping the work straight is to miss the first stitch of the row and to work a stitch into the top turning chain of the previous row. Always check the number of stitches every row until it automatically becomes even with the edges straight.

Increasing inc

Gradual Increasing to Make a Curve
Work two stitches into one space. The turning chain counts as the first stitch so the increase has to be on the second stitch. At the end of the row increase by working two stitches into one space on the last stitch but one.

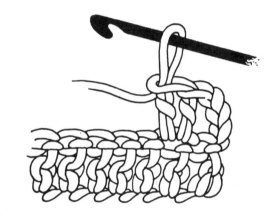

Fig 63

Increasing a Number of Stitches at Once
At the beginning of the row Deduct one from the number of stitches you wish to add in chains plus the number of turning chain for the stitch being used. For example, if the stitch being used was treble and five more stitches were needed, then 4+3tch=7ch. Seven chain would give an increase of five trebles.
At the end of the row Attach a spare piece of yarn to the previous row and work a number of chain. Crochet across the row and use the spare chain at the end to make the number of stitches you wish to increase. Unpick the spare chain not required.

Decreasing dec

Gradual Decreasing to Make a Curve

It is possible just to miss a stitch but often this is not very satisfactory as it makes a hole. The best way to decrease is to work whatever stitch you are using until there are two loops left on the hook, then work the next stitch to the same stage so there will be three loops on the hook. Yarn round hook and work the three loops together. Work in this manner at the beginning of the row after the turning chain and on the second and third stitch before the last stitch at the end of the row.

Decreasing a Number of Stitches at Once

At the beginning of the row Use a slip stitch to travel along the work the number of necessary stitches, take one more slip stitch and work the standing chain. Check that you have decreased the required number.

At the end of the row Crochet along the row and leave the required number of stitches unworked. Make the turning chain for the next row and turn.

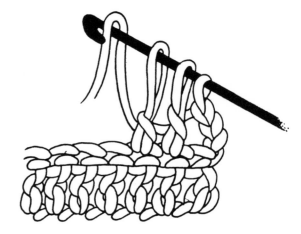

Fig 64

APPENDIX 2

USE OF SYMBOLS

Symbols are a diagrammatic way of writing crochet. Although they are not yet generally used for crochet patterns, I have included information about them as they will become more widely accepted. Those who can crochet but find difficulty in reading a pattern may find it much easier to follow a chart of symbols.

While it can be difficult to write crochet patterns and often difficult to understand what the designer actually means, this system of symbols is an international language, as readily followed in Tokyo as in Europe. Many European and Japanese magazines are using this diagrammatic way of writing patterns but they are not yet generally accepted in Britain and the United States. The patterns are easy to follow if the basic stitches and their symbols are known.

Tunisian symbols are given in the French book *Tricot Selection* (see Appendix 4). No symbols for Broomstick Crochet have yet been evolved.

General Guidelines

Figures indicate the rows.
Letters A B C etc indicate changes of colours.
Arrows indicate the direction of the work.
The symbols are self-explanatory:
eg 2 trebles into 1 st is an increase
 2 stitches worked together is a decrease
The bar on the treble sign illustrates the number of times the wool is put round the hook for the stitch. American terms have one yarn over less.

	UK		USA	
⬭	chain	ch	chain	ch
⬬	slip stitch	sl st	slip stitch	sl st
+	double crochet	dc	single crochet	sc
T	half treble	htr	half double crochet	hdc
Ŧ	treble	tr	double crochet	dc
₮	double treble	dtr	treble	tr
₮	triple treble	tr tr	double treble	dtr
₮	quadruple treble	quad tr	triple treble	tr tr
₮	quintuple treble	quin tr	quadruple treble	quad tr
₮	sextuple treble	sex tr	quintuple treble	quin tr

109

Decreasing and Increasing to Form Groups and Clusters

		UK		USA	
⋈	2	double crochet	dc	single crochet	sc
♠	3				
⋀	2	half treble	htr	half double crochet	hdc
⋀	3				
⬚	3				
⬚	4				
⬚	5				
⋀	2	treble	tr	double crochet	dc
⋀	3				
⬚	3				
⬚	4				
⬚	5				
⋀	2	double treble	dtr	treble	tr
⋀	3				
⬚	4				
⬚	5				
⋀	5				
⋀	2	triple treble	tr tr	double treble	dtr
⋀	3				
⋀	5				
⋀	9				

Design 22: Dramatic evening coat with very full sleeves (page 96)

Tunisian Crochet Symbols

		UK			USA	
I	Tunisian simple		Ts		Tunisian simple or Afghan stitch	Ts
~	return row				return row	
—	Tunisian purl		Tp		Tunisian purl	Tp
T	Tunisian half treble		Tht		Tunisian half treble	Tht
 ⱦ	Tunisian treble		Ttr		Tunisian treble	Ttr
 ⱦ	Tunisian double treble		Tdtr		Tunisian double treble	Tdtr
�9	Tunisian stitch double		Td			

The bottom of the symbol indicates where the hook should go:

ʃ round the stem of the stitch – raised treble front (RtrF)

ʅ round the back of the stitch – raised treble back (RtrB)

J through the stitch

Design 25: Thick blanket made on a rug-length broomstick (page 101)

HOOK SIZES

UK	US		UK	US
0.60mm	14 steel		4.00mm	F
0.75mm	12 steel		4.50mm	G
1.00mm	10 steel		5.00mm	H
1.25mm	8 steel		5.50mm	H
1.50mm	7 steel		6.00mm	I
1.75mm	4 steel		7.00mm	K
2.00mm	0		8.00mm	11 wood
2.50mm	B		9.00mm	13 wood
3.00mm	C		10.00mm	15 wood
3.50mm	E			

APPENDIX 4

EQUIPMENT

Basic Materials
A selection of hooks of different sizes
Yarns of different textures

In Addition You Will Need
Tunisian hooks
Large needles for Broomstick Crochet
Hairpins

To Measure
A tape measure with inches on one side and centimetres on the other
A ruler

Sewing Up
Large wool needles
Bodkin

Pins with glass knobs

Pressing
Iron
Pressing surface (large old table) prepared with thick blanket and cover
Pressing cloth of cotton or muslin
Sleeve board
Padded shapes

Pattern Making
Cutting scissors
Large sheets of paper
Calculator
Notebook
Pencil and felt-tip pens

APPENDIX 5

LIST OF SUPPLIERS

Wool Firms
J. & P. Coats, Crochet Suppliers
15 Vincent Street
Glasgow
Scotland

Patons & Baldwins
PO Box
McMullen Road
Darlington
Co Durham BL1 1YQ

Sirdar
Flansham Lane
Alverthorpe
Wakefield
W Yorks WF2 9ND

Rowan Yarns
Green Lane
Washpit
Holmfirth
W Yorks

Scheepjeswol
7 Colemeadow Road
PO Box 48
Redditch
Worcs B98 9NZ

Scheepjeswol USA Inc
155 Lafayette Ave
North White Plains
NY 10603

Georges Picaud of Paris
c/o Priory Yarns Ltd
48 Station Road
Ossett
W Yorks

H. G. Twilley Ltd
Roman Mill
Stamford
Lincs PE9 1B6

Phildar (UK) Ltd
4 Gambrel Road
Westgate Industrial Estate
Northampton NN5 5NF

Wool Shops
There are very good wool shops in nearly every town.
Some sell hand-spun, hand-dyed, locally-produced
yarns which are beautiful. Listed below are the shops I
have found, but there are many more. Those marked *
have a good selection of hand-spun, hand-dyed yarn.

UK
*Creativity
45 New Oxford Street
London WC1
and
15 Downing Street
Farnham
Surrey
Goods available by mail order from the Farnham
address

Colourway
112a Westbourne Grove
London W2

Ries Wools
242 High Holborn
London WC1

Shepherds Purse and Meadows
2 St John Street
Bath

Bobbins
Wesley Hall
Church Street
Whitby
N Yorks

Up Country
Towngate
Holmfirth
W Yorks

116

Designer Yarns
367 Sauchiehall Street
Glasgow G2
Scotland

Siop Jen
91 Pontcanna Street
Cardiff
Wales

*Ray Napier
54 Neal Street
Covent Garden
London WC2

Patricia Roberts
31 St James Street
Covent Garden
London WC2

The Black Sheep Shop
Aylsham
Norfolk

Handywoman Knitting Yarns
105 Chiswick High Road
London W4 2ED

Designer Wools
Ray Napier
54 Neal Street
Covent Garden
London WC2

*Gloria Watson
Dorset Yarns & Dyes
Manor Farm Cottage
West Stour
Near Gillingham
Dorset

The Sheep Dip
57 Fore Street
Bovey Tracey
Devon

USA
Fiber Works
313 East 45th Street
New York

Straw with Gold
3006 San Pablo Avenue
Berkeley
California

Soft Spectrum
216 Grand Avenue
Pacific Grove
California

Dyed in the Wool Ltd
252 West 37th Street
Suite 1800
New York 10018

Herrschners
Hoover Road
Stevens Point
Wisconsin 54481

Fiber Folio
11 West 37th Street
New York 10018

Tunisian Hooks
Creativity (see Wool Shops for address)

The Crochet Design Centre
White Cross
Lancaster LA1 4XH

Scheepjeswol (see Wool Firms for address)

Aero Needles Group PLC
PO Box 2
Edward Street
Redditch
Worcs B97 6HB

Henry Milward & Sons
Arrow Works
Studley
Warwicks B80 7AS

Double-ended Tunisian hooks are only available from Creativity and The Crochet Design Centre.

Hand-made Wooden Hooks
Twin Birch Products
PO Box 50W
Winslow
Maine 04902
USA

Broomsticks
M. E. Kent
1 Orchard Street
Chichester
W Sussex PO19 1DD

The Crochet Design Centre
(see Tunisian Hooks for address)

APPENDIX 5: LIST OF SUPPLIERS

Buttons
Pottery Buttons
Jane Smith
5 Acorn Street
Keswick
Cumbria

Wooden Buttons
Robin Maddock
25 Chessel Avenue
Southampton SO2 4DY

Norwegian Metal Buttons and Jacket Fastenings
Creativity (see Wool Shops for address)

Horn Buttons
Abbey Horn of Kendal
The Horn Shop
Stricklandgate
Kendal
Cumbria

Beads
The Honourable Bead
The Emporium
Tarrant Street
Arundel
W Sussex

The Bead Shop
Neal Street
Covent Garden
London W2

Books
Tricot Selection: 1400 Points de Tricot de Crochet et de Crochet Tunisian, imported from France only by Mrs C. Beaumont, 5 Scarborough Road, Lytham St Anne's, Lancs FY8 3ER. Includes many Tunisian stitches, but explanations are in symbols only.
A Complete Crochet Course by Muriel Kent, David & Charles.
Broomstick Crochet, WI Books Limited.
Slip Knot, The Knitting & Crochet Guild. Available from Mrs E. Gillett, 5 Roman Mount, Leeds L88 2DD.

ACKNOWLEDGEMENTS

I would like to thank all those people who helped with the preparation of the book, especially Lyn Blake of Line Design who prepared the illustrations; J. & P. Coats Ltd for their kind permission to copy the hand positions in Figs 1, 2, 3 & 4 and some of the stitch diagrams from *Learn to Crochet 1292*; Marjorie Eden for typing the manuscript; Grace Deakin for her cross stitch embroidery; Clive Royston of Priory Yarns; Dave & Mary Vinall of Flying Colours, Chichester; the yarn firms of Priory Yarns, Scheepjeswol (UK) Ltd and Rowan Yarns who kindly donated materials for some of the garments.

My thanks also to Pam Griffiths, my editor, who was always patient, and Tony Griffiths for his interpretative photography. The publishers would particularly like to thank R. C. Austin Ltd of Newton Abbot for their generous help in loaning all the accessories for photography.

INDEX

INDEX